THE PAIN OF PASTORING
What Every Pastor Wants You To Know

RODERICK RICHARSON, M.s.,M.Ed.

RICH ENTERPRISES *LLC*

The Pain of Pastoring

By

Roderick Richardson

©2020 Rich Enterprises, LLC

Rich Enterprises, LLC

1888 Main St. Ste. C #255

Madison, MS 39110

All scripture verses marked NASB are taken from the New American Standard Bible. Used by permission.

Library of Congress Cataloging-in-Publication Data

Edited by

Published by Rich Enterprises, LLC

Library of Congress Control Number: 9780997745627

ISBN: 978-0-9977456-4-1 (print)

ISBN: 978-1-09831-229-9 (ebook)

10 9 8 7 6 5 4 3 2 1

Printed in the United States of America.

Note: This book is intended only as an informative guide for those experiencing the pastorate. Names have been changed to protect the integrity of the stories. The reader is advised to read for personal consumption and not use for research purposes. The reader assumes all responsibility for the consequences of any actions taken based on the information presented in this book. The information in this book relies on the author's and fellow cohorts' experience. Every attempt has been made to ensure that the data is accurate; however, the author cannot accept liability for any errors that may exist. The facts and stories within the confines of the book are subject to interpretation, and the conclusions and recommendations presented here may not agree with other interpretations.

Dedication

To my God. You've shown yourself mighty in my life. You are the light during my darkest moments. You're a cheerleader even when no one is in the stands. I'll forever serve you!

To the two ladies that keep me anchored, my wife and daughter. Thank you for your patience and understanding in sharing me with the world. I dedicate this book to you.

To my deceased mother. I wish that you were here to see your beautiful granddaughter and what has become of your lineage. I hope to make you proud as I forge through the vicissitudes of life.

To my deceased grandmother. You were the Mr. Miyagi in my life. I followed you to church every week. I saw you navigate the politics and church drama while being a faithful musician. You taught me patience, grace, and forgiveness. I'll never forget it.

To my stepfather. I am forever grateful. Without you, I wouldn't have had the exposure to the world that helped frame my paradigm. I am forever grateful!

To my church. Thank you for entrusting me to be your pastor. Thank you for your prayers, support, and your faithfulness to the principles of the Holy Bible. I love you dearly!

Contents

INTRODUCTION

Listed as one of the toughest professions known to man. There is no clock to punch, your supervisor is God, your accountability is a board of directors, and your office space is the world. No one can articulate the pain associated with pastoring like one who has pastored. I've been in ministry for twenty-one years and pastoring for a decade. *The Pain of Pastoring* is not a collection of statistics, yet there are some statistics. This book is not just a collection of stories of others. The majority of what's in the confines of this book are events, situations that I've seen with my eyes, heard with my ears, and experienced with my heart.

The reason I wrote this book is to tell the story from our perspective. Pastors are silent, not because they want to be, but because the pain of pastoring can be so intolerable that the agony often cannot be uttered with words. All too often, we see a Pastor fall, or the Pastor's lifestyle comes to light, and the public judges the Pastor for the results, but never stops to question "how did he or she get there?" Additionally, we have come to live in a society where the church is a punching bag for the people she helps care for, cover, correct, and console. We are quick to forget the late calls to pray, the hospital visits, the burial of family members, consolation during tough times, or the wisdom given on a whim. Pastors have to be well versed theologically, economically, sociologically, politically, and educationally, among other disciplines, because the church is the first place people seek wisdom. We are often counselors, confidants, and caregivers. When light bills are in arrears, they call the Pastor. When relationships falter, they call the pastor. When the eviction notices come, they call the Pastor. Pastors are often required to give a return to people who rarely invest. We are often the subject of ridicule, lies, slander, and merely unfair treatment. Enough is enough! It's time to bare all.

WHO SHOULD READ THIS BOOK?

This book is for everyone. This book is for the ministry leader who serves God through the local church. The ministry leader differs from a regular parishioner because he or she often has the opportunity to see the Pastor when they are not at their best. Yes, the Pastor has mood swings. Sometimes life hits them. Many Pastors have financial issues and other issues just like parishioners.

This book is for the parishioner who follows diligently and requires more of their Pastor than they are willing to demand from themselves. Pastors pay parishioners bills while their own bills go delinquent. Those who have larger churches with payrolls often have to wait to get paid so that everyone else can enjoy the fruits of their labor, yet many complain that he or she has a Pastor's Anniversary each year. Whatever that anniversary check comes to be is often "catch-up" for falling behind. This book is for parishioners who need their Pastor to be healthy emotionally and spiritually. A parishioner can come into the Pastor's office and tell them all types of freaky stuff, but when they hear the Pastor has a shortcoming, they disappear like Houdini or judge them like they're "the People's Court."

The Pain of Pastoring

The Pain of Pastoring is for the world of people who don't subscribe to the church or the gospel. Some believe that pastoring is an easy hustle. You see a few abusive ones and judge the entire vocation. While I'm writing this book, there is a salmonella outbreak in twenty-six states among various foods. I'm sure millions saw it on the news, but it didn't stop them from eating food. It's only in the church where you stop wanting to receive from it when there is an isolated outbreak. These same individuals believe that all a Pastor does is collect money. All Wal-Mart wants is our money, but we keep going back. The church needs money to operate effectively. I dedicate this book to opening your eyes and enlightening you to a world of abuse and neglect that a Pastor receives while walking in the integrity of God.

Lastly, this book is for every person whom God has called to the office of the Pastorate. It is for those who have the grace and calling to press forward, all while hurting. *The Pain of Pastoring* is for those who want to quit every week to keep from dealing with ungrateful people. It's for the Pastors who are barely holding their households together because the church has become their mistress. It's for the Pastor who drinks himself or herself to sleep and engages in unbecoming behavior because there is not an expansion valve to release the pain associated with a pastoral discipline. This is for the bi-vocational Pastor who has to juggle both their job and Jesus. You give countless hours only to be slandered, backstabbed, and abused at the hands of those you're called to help. This book is for you!

This book is for every young Pastor who thinks he or she will start a church without any stress or duress—the young visionaries who believe that when they open the church, Heaven will open. *The Pain of Pastoring* is for the ones who aren't prepared for the barrage of attacks associated with doing kingdom. Let this book be a warning as well as enlightenment to the siege and war waged on Pastors and the church at large. Let it be your introductory class in the hard knocks of ministry. This book is for you!

My aim is not to be diplomatic in this body of work but to deliver stark truths. These truths are shared by a fraternity of brothers and sisters across the world. My aim is to separate many from the cognitive dissonance that pastoring is easy and some fly-by profession. I want to give readers the notion that all Pastors are not "paid," and have not made it on Easy Street. I want to deliver those reading this book from thinking that the Pastor is Superman. I want to introduce you to the Clark Kents. I want to challenge you and change your mind about the pastorate. I promise to give it to you straight with no chaser!

I CAN'T GET NO SATISFACTION

We must all suffer one of two things: the pain of discipline or the pain of regret or disappointment.

— Jim Rohn

At the time of writing this book, the world is uneasy. I'm receiving hundreds of messages in my inbox saying Pastor, we love you, and we are praying for you and your family. There is an alarm at the gate for shepherds across the country. Why the sudden concern for the shepherd?

Shepherds have always provided a vital role in people's lives.

NO DOUBT PEOPLE LOVE THEIR PASTOR, BUT IT'S OFTEN NOT OVERTLY EXPRESSED ON A REGULAR BASIS EXCEPT THOUGH OCCASIONAL SPECIAL SERVICES

No doubt people love their Pastor, but it's often not overtly expressed on a regular basis except though occasional special services. Currently, the world is at attention because of the news that a young mega-church Pastor took his own life. Seemly, the young Pastor had everything to look forward to, including a beautiful church with a large budget, an internationally recognized brand, a prospering family, and unwavering influence. He had ninety-nine problems, and money wasn't one, yet he chose to take his own life. Could it be that the world is shocked at his age, which was the ripe young age of thirty? Could it be that it was revealed that he was currently in a series about depression and sadness yet suffering from the same ailments he preached to other people? Maybe it was the fact that people were shocked that he had personal issues.

The expectancy of people to think that the Pastor has no kryptonite is quite common. The Pastor, like others, are ordinary people with extraordinary gifts.

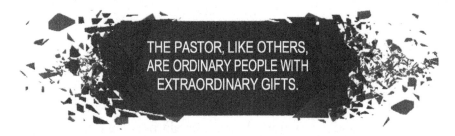

THE PASTOR, LIKE OTHERS, ARE ORDINARY PEOPLE WITH EXTRAORDINARY GIFTS.

They place their pants on one leg at a time, just like those listening from the pews. They bleed the same blood. They hurt the same way, and life challenges them as well. The only difference between Pastors and the rest of the congregation is that we have to lead others while bleeding ourselves. Although I advocate for being spiritually healthy, often Pastors have too small a budget to get away and heal while someone assumes responsibility. As a result, they have to stick close to the ministry and ultimately end up impacting their families and their congregation by smothering them with the blood from their wounds. The people they preach to are getting better, but the Pastor becomes a casualty to the process of others' healing. So by the time the parishioners get well, the teachers themselves need healing.

JONAH

When a person first starts a church, they are naïve, like I was. They think their friends will support them, strangers will come, and families will assist in building and advocating for their cause. I learned quickly that whatever is moving becomes a target, and whoever motivates you to start often doesn't have the money to help you get going. You become a target of attracting people who are looking for opportunities. They know the Pastor will be looking for a music minister. The church will be looking for ministers and assistants. People will attempt to marry your potential with their opportunity. If they feel you will have an inkling of anointing and momentum, they will jump on the boat and weigh it down with dead cargo. Jonah weighed down a cargo ship because of disobedience. Jonahs have a purpose, but everyone called is not called to be on your boat. As a result, Pastors lose vital cargo because of unprofitable weight. They shouldn't be on your boat. When you grow as fast as our church did, it facilitated a significant need. People sniff out new Pastors' needs like a wolf hunting for evening dinner. You think people who joined you have your heart's interest, but they are after what's in your hand. They are looking for you to lift them up and share the platform that God has given you. They don't want your wisdom or words. They want a "way." They want a way up, a way out, and a way to. These individuals will stick with you long enough to see if you're going to win. If they are close to you, they will benefit from the spoils you gain from conquering challenges. Should there be a sign of trouble, they will literally jump into the enormous fish mouth to abort the mission they said they were supposed to support.

THE CALL

One of the stories that surfaced during coverage of the young Pastor is that he succeeded his father in ministry. Often times, we forget due to do the occupational pull that Pastoring is a spiritual vocation as well. Many times, a zealous young minister picks up a microphone and thinks that speaking is all it takes to pastor people. Ministry is much more consuming and takes much more than eloquent elocution! When God called the disciples during his earlier journey, they were professionals. Andrew was a commercial fisherman when he met Jesus. Mathew was a tax collector, and Luke was a doctor. Note how Jesus called upon them to drop their occupation to follow him. If it was possible to do ministry at the highest level part-time, then the disciples would have done both while learning from Jesus. This is not to say that one is not doing real ministry while being bi-vocational, but it lends the narrative that ministry done right takes full-time energy.

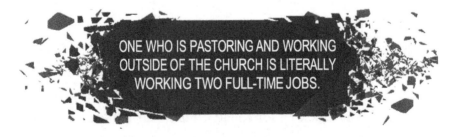

ONE WHO IS PASTORING AND WORKING OUTSIDE OF THE CHURCH IS LITERALLY WORKING TWO FULL-TIME JOBS.

One who is pastoring and working outside of the church is literally working two full-time jobs. They have to divide their loyalty to what they've been called to do and what they have to do to keep their households afloat. Each job takes a considerable amount of energy. Each one is important. Depending on the pull from the family or the ministry, it's easy for a Pastor to get out of balance and become a victim to the lack of margin it takes to stay healthy spiritually, mentally, emotionally, financially, and physically.

HE EQUIPS WHO HE CALLS

The calling is crucial. It's vital because God equips who He calls. If you're called to sing, then God equips you with a voice. If you're called to be a surgeon, God equips you with decent eyes and steady hands. If he calls you to be a lawyer, He provides you with the uncanny ability to lie. (I'm just joking!) Your purpose is always an answer to a problem.

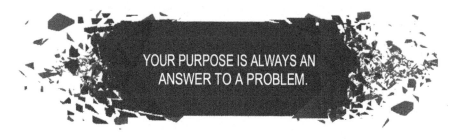

YOUR PURPOSE IS ALWAYS AN
ANSWER TO A PROBLEM.

If you're the answer to a problem, then you'll have the necessary equipment to help solve that problem.

God's equipping is much like a painter having a brush, a carpenter having a hammer, a singer having a voice, or a lawyer having logic. Although anyone can buy a stick, use logic, try to sing, or pick up a brush from the local Home Depot, when you have been called to something, you'll excel in using what's in your hands, ingrained in your heart, or lingering on your lips.

Across the country, people through their own volition have stepped into an arena in which they are not adequately equipped. God's promise of protection often followed commands of obedience. If a person is not in purpose, they won't fall under God's auspices of security and prosperity. In church terms, we would say that a person is anointed for the job. To explain to those who may not be familiar with those terms, Isaiah Chapter ten talks about burdens being lifted and yokes destroyed because of the anointing. In essence, the anointing gives you God's ability, including but not limited to wisdom, to remove stuff that entangles with us spiritually, emotionally, or existentially. When God calls those to the pastorate, He gives the ability to handle the hardships of ministry.

You may ask, then why write the book? It comes with the territory. You, in essence, are equipped if you say you're called, right?

Yes, but there are unnecessary frivolities we have to battle that those outside the calling need to be aware of. It is challenging to build a house, while the one you're paying to work is stealing your bricks. We are being abused without parishioners noticing. We are being taken for granted. We are experiencing unnecessary pain at the hands of people we are called to pastor. We are being bitten by the sheep that we help free from the jaws of the lurking wolves.

WHEN GOD SAYS NO

David had desired to build the Kingdom. God declared to him, because of the blood on his hands, he wouldn't be the instrument to construct his greatest desire. God had to tell him no. Instead, he let his son Solomon build a state-of-the-art facility. I feel like David sometimes. I moved to Jackson, Mississippi, to attend one of the local law schools. It had always been in my heart to become a lawyer. I had it all planned. I was going to go to law school, open a firm, and sue Disney. That's right. Sue Disney. I knew just by their presentation that their employment structure was unfair to people of color. Lo and behold, I was right. Years later, a renowned lawyer by the name of Willie Gary sued them for over a billion dollars and won. I would have been set for life!

I mention this narrative because, like many other Pastors, I had ambitions to do something else. I didn't go into ministry because it was ideal. I didn't go into ministry because I thought it was an easy way to garner income. I always operated at a high level in my prospective disciplines. With four degrees, I could easily do other things. I was drafted. Pastoring was the furthest thing from my mind, and I was under the impression that a call into ministry was a call into poverty. Where I am from in Mississippi, we had no clue about the mega-ministries and the few television Pastors who live comfortable lives. Just to make it clear, there is nothing wrong with having a great living from the fruits of your labor. My motives were pure. I was upset, yet I yielded to the call. I left my dreams and aspirations of the legal field and entrepreneurship for the ministry. I had options, but I chose the one that God had called me to. God had said no to what I wanted, so I said yes to His will!

UNSETTLED

The church climate has definitely changed. Looking at the declining roles and church participation, thousands of churches close their doors each year. Barna Research Group, in partnership with Pepperdine University, prepared a study entitled "The State of Pastors." The authors stated, "This study offers great insights into the hearts, minds, and daily reality of those who lead our churches. In the end, we are encouraged by what we see in the findings. The pulpits of our churches are occupied by creative, passionate Pastors who love God and desire to see the Church thrive in the days ahead. But behind the hopeful signs are hints of weariness. The margin for some of our Pastors is paper-thin."

The research group compared the state of the Pastors to being paper-thin and weary. They examined the support systems, study habits, the burdens of the pastorate, and provided viable solutions. They question the workload, the preparation, and the mental health of those who lead their institutions. Some of the unsettling results include the following:

- One out of every four Pastors had experienced a period during their ministry when they significantly doubted their faith.

- Forty-three percent of Pastors are at high or medium risk, whether they are experiencing challenges in marriage, family, friendships, or other close relationships.

- One in five Pastors has struggled with an addiction—most commonly, to alcohol while almost half-faced depression.

- Most Pastors are faring well, but one in three is at risk of burnout.

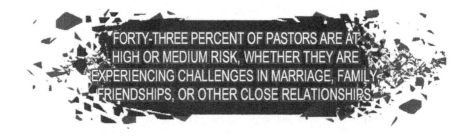

FORTY-THREE PERCENT OF PASTORS ARE AT HIGH OR MEDIUM RISK, WHETHER THEY ARE EXPERIENCING CHALLENGES IN MARRIAGE, FAMILY, FRIENDSHIPS, OR OTHER CLOSE RELATIONSHIPS

Are you alarmed? The statistics are staggering, but this is only a glance at what Pastors face on a regular basis. The average Pastor makes less than twenty thousand dollars a year, yet their education attainment calls for more than double that. Nearly seventy-five percent of Pastors have to hold down another job. Imagine what you currently do at work in addition to having to be concerned about fifty, hundred, two hundred fifty, five hundred, or thousand others God entrusts in your care. I know it's overwhelming, and the average parishioner and ministry worker have no clue. It unsettling that a Pastor could be counseling on a topic that they have not conquered themselves. Pride is often the culprit that disallows them to refer you to someone else.

For this reason, every Pastor needs a Pastor. Dr. R.A. Vernon says, "Don't tell me who you are over until you tell me who you are under." Every Pastor needs an outlet.

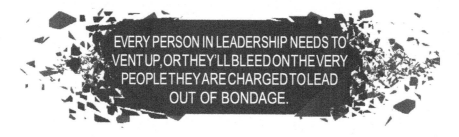

EVERY PERSON IN LEADERSHIP NEEDS TO VENT UP, OR THEY'LL BLEED ON THE VERY PEOPLE THEY ARE CHARGED TO LEAD OUT OF BONDAGE.

Every person in leadership needs to vent up, or they'll bleed on the very people they are charged to lead out of bondage. Until we recognize that our Pastors are under undying pressure, we will continue to lose Pastors to wrong decisions, burnout, and untimely death.

FEELING THE PINCH

Pastors are getting older. The average age of a Pastor is forty-four to fifty-five. With the aging population of teachers, the gaps are widening between the generations. There is a defying pressure to reach back. I often echo to Pastors who I mentor and cover that "anything without youth has no future." Those in ministry know the undying pressure to get and keep a connection with the crowd. Some may call this phenomenon momentum. Momentum is hard to understand and easy to lose.

When you have it, you must ride the wave until God or the culture places you in retirement. Pastors who have experienced growth understand that they will not always be as influential. People are less likely to join in droves. As soon as the Pastor does something they don't like, they trade him in like an older-model car. Whether Pastors admit it, we're fighting to be relevant in people's lives. Going beyond just good teaching, Pastors struggle for creativity through new titles, object lessons, and cunning stories. We have to research so that we won't date ourselves during sermons by using outdated linguistics. One can often find unseasoned Pastors misusing or slaughtering a colloquialism to appear cool and connected. Because of the advent of social media, the Pastor's faux pas is often encapsulated in time and replayed to millions when social media posts go viral.

RELEVANT OR NOT?

The struggle for relevance wasn't always an important issue. However, we are a generation inundated with options. The strength of loyalty is often tested in the face of possibilities. Dr. Dharius Daniels once said, "You can't say you're loyal until you had a chance not to be." It wasn't always this way. Church culture, when I was growing up, was where you were baptized, married, and buried. One would even have burial plots because the church had sections of land reserved to honor its dead. People were faithful. They were loyal and committed to the cause. They could disagree with leadership and still be led by them.

We're in a time where correction equals separation. When the Pastor corrects a person, instead of them making an adjustment, they make a move. People will go to smoother waters because your correction is interpreted as confrontation. The younger generation will dismiss your unction to correct as hate, yet you're fighting for them. You're struggling to sift through this culture for ways to reach them. You're searching for ways to keep connected with the ancient liturgies. You want them to know God. You want them to experience God. However, pastoring in the twenty-first century is like Moses leading the Israelites out of Egypt. They are fighting against him while he is helping them. Pay attention as I mention stories about people who fought the very people that threw them a life preserver.

WE'RE IN A TIME WHERE CORRECTION EQUALS SEPARATION.

YOUR LAST SERMON

One of my mentors would often echo the sentiment, "Son, you're only as strong as your last sermon." Interpreted in many ways, one can construe that people have short memories. We can also infer that people don't give you many chances to make first impressions. As a Pastor, you have to always be on your "A" game. If you're not on your "A" game, then you'd better act like it.

The pressure to preach is real. People don't understand what it takes to construct a message. Dr. R.A. Vernon, in his book *Help, My Pastor is Under Pressure*, said, "Every week, usually twice a week, Pastors must come up with something to say that doesn't put folk to sleep. They have to tell the same old stories in fresh new ways." How many times can you hear the Christmas story? On Resurrection Sunday, you know how the story ends. As a result, we have to resort to creative means to give people fresh spiritual food. Pastors like myself, Dr. Daniels, and

Dr. Vernon, are Pastors who avidly read books. Books provide meaty materials for well-constructed sermons. For those who are required to prepare sermons on a regular basis, I suggest that you step outside of the Holy text and read various perspectives. It will expand your intellectual weaponry and shift your paradigm.

Additionally, I personally subscribe to Logos, which is one of the world's largest Bible software providers. Inundated with information beyond comprehension—books, current events, social justice issues, existential issues, personal issues, family issues, leadership issues, theological constructs, and just the vicissitudes of life—the Pastor's mind is consumed with information, and none of it is without significance. The overarching problem is that running minds often lead to sketchy decisions. We often find ourselves struggling to try to mentally prioritize what we need, what people need, and what God requires.

WE OFTEN FIND OURSELVES STRUGGLING TO TRY TO MENTALLY PRIORITIZE WHAT WE NEED, WHAT PEOPLE NEED, AND WHAT GOD REQUIRES.

PAID VERSUS PIMPING

Pastors put in a lot of work. According to Thom Rainer, well-known church consultant, eighty-seven percent of Pastors work more than forty hours a week, and more than sixty percent work sixty hours or more. These stats were without regard to the vocational status of the Pastor. Some Pastors have full-time jobs and still work up to sixty hours a week. Those of you reading this book, if you put in sixty hours of anything, you would expect to get paid. The truth is that many Pastors invest that much into a ministry that can't yield half of what they are worth. Ministry is an investment where the return is often not tangible. When there are returns, and people begin to see the tangible results of the Pastor's toil, they may say the Pastor somehow manipulated or stole to get it. This is the fallacy committed by those standing on the outside. To the world, they are pimps and grew off the backs of the people despite the providence of divine favor and good ole hard work.

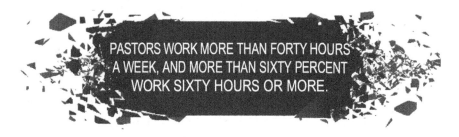

PASTORS WORK MORE THAN FORTY HOURS A WEEK, AND MORE THAN SIXTY PERCENT WORK SIXTY HOURS OR MORE.

INVESTMENT

When we started our ministry, we started from scratch. Growing up in the Deep South, the word "scratch" had a different connotation. My grandmother would make biscuits or cornbread from scratch. Scratch meant that she only had the raw ingredients, and it was up to her to combine those ingredients to make a finished product. There weren't pre-made mixes bought from the store, only raw ingredients. Many younger people don't understand what it takes to build something because they are a "Jiffy Mix" generation. When we started our ministry, we began with the raw ingredients. We weren't transitional, meaning we weren't an established church with a board, budget, and bucks. Our budget was relegated to what we had saved personally. We had to fund everything. We had to buy mics, sound equipment, nursery equipment, parking equipment, children's church equipment, and anything else you could imagine it would take to start something. On top of the startup equipment, we signed contracts on the strength of our names and become the guarantors for properties because banks don't usually do business with new entities. The church didn't have a track record. We had to bleed capital. When something was due, and there wasn't enough money in the church account, we had to write the check from our personal savings. All businessmen reading this book understand this concept. There are many acceptable accounting principles Pastors and boards have to know. In churches, you have profit-and-loss statements, balance sheets, and other vital accounting information to determine the financial health of a church. Like business, many churches won't see any real surplus of cash flow until about the second or third year. If this is the case, who do the expenses fall upon? I know Pastors who have destroyed or stretched their credit to capacity caring for the church. I know Pastors who have had to file bankruptcy because of the church. Although it doesn't make what they did right, it does accentuate burdens outside of what the average parishioner understands that Pastors have to face.

THE JOHN GRAY EFFECT

During the birthing of this book, one of my favorite Pastors was in the news, for all the wrong reasons. Pastor Gray, a protégé of one of the most effective Pastors in the world, Joel Osteen, became the successor of Ron Carpenter. He inherited thousands of members and a state-of-the-art building. Pastor Carpenter didn't give Gray a platform. He was already mainstream and conducting weekly Wednesday night service for Pastor Osteen. He had traveled the world preaching, teaching, and bringing laughter to the saints of all nationalities, ages, and socioeconomic statuses. On top of his ministerial success, Pastor Gray has a successful reality series on the Oprah Network. To add icing on the cake, he is a two-time best-selling author. Pastor Gray has garnered millions. He is on the path to be one of our twenty-first-century generals of the gospel. One cannot deny his tangible anointing and undeniable success. Recently, Pastor Gray celebrated a marital milestone in his marriage to Pastor Aventer. During the celebration, someone snapped a picture of the gift he gave his wife for their anniversary. The image made its way to social media and eventually went viral, especially among the "church" community. It didn't take the "undefeated" internet to launch vicious assaults for buying his wife a Lamborghini for this momentous milestone. The car, estimated to be worth over two-hundred-thousand dollars, became the conversation on social media, talk shows, and behind closed doors. It sounds like a lot of money, doesn't it? To most people, it is a lot of money, but for someone who has a reality show on the wealthiest African American woman's network, best-selling books, salary from the largest church in America, money from speaking engagements, and other business endeavors that are not public, I beg to differ. Many of the comments online included, "Why give these mega-churches your money so they can live lavishly?" "Pastor Gray bought that car with church money." Really? I will go on record guessing that Pastor Gray's finances are probably more in-depth and in better condition than the church he inherited. "Well, he benefited from the church." Don't you benefit from your job? If you work at AT&T, you receive a discount from helping customers. He, like many other Pastors, is being penalized for making better life decisions than most people. Coupled with the favor of God in his life, and multiple business endeavors, why can't he buy what he wants? Is it because he is a Pastor? Is it because a community of believers doesn't like him? Or, is it because many don't have finances to make such a purchase? I believe you wouldn't be a happy camper if others legislate how you spend your money. Why legislate how he or anyone else spend theirs?

PERSPECTIVE

If a young CEO builds its company from zero to two-thousand, four-thousand, or ten-thousand employees, the world calls them a genius. It's only in the pastorate that when a Pastor grows to exceed the church norms, that brings an uncomfortable wave of criticism from a one-sided perspective. A good friend of mine recently bought a house. An unsuspected lurker went downtown to retrieve the public record of this well-known Pastor. He utilized this information to create a social media blast that went viral in his city. He touted that this young Pastor, who was barely thirty-five at the time, had a nine-hundred-thousand-dollar home in an upscale part of his town. Does this sound like gross negligence to you? Stop! Let's review the entire situation. This young Pastor had grown his church in a short nine-year period to over ten-thousand members with a weekly attendance of over three thousand. He has one of the most progressive ministries in the country. He has a conference each year that draws over five-thousand women with no guest psalmist or guest preachers. He is an author of multiple books. Why can't he have a house of his liking? If what he has done is so easy, try it. What a Pastor buys with his salary is his business. He has five children and needs more space than the average person. A young CEO who grows his company to be a multi-million-dollar conglomerate is celebrated among his peers. A young Pastor replicates results in a different arena, and he is a pimp. According to popular opinion, he is prostituting the people to afford a lifestyle they can only dream of. The story of my friend is one told all too often. I teach Pastors with larger churches to place their homes in a silent trust. Hide your privacy. Delete yourself from the search engines to protect the hearts of people who can't handle the favor.

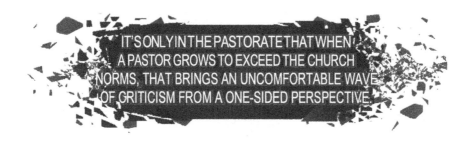

IT'S ONLY IN THE PASTORATE THAT WHEN A PASTOR GROWS TO EXCEED THE CHURCH NORMS, THAT BRINGS AN UNCOMFORTABLE WAVE OF CRITICISM FROM A ONE-SIDED PERSPECTIVE.

The sentiments mentioned above echo the fact that Pastors are misunderstood. It's hard to get satisfaction when people believe that somehow every Pastor has to take a vow of poverty. Sorry, that's the Catholic Church. I serve a God that has pleasure when His servant does well spiritually and existentially. I have to ask what type of car your Pastor should drive? What kind of house should your Pastor live in? What kind of clothing should they wear? What is too much or too little? Is your life the barometer to his blessings? They can have beautiful things as long as they're not as lovely as yours, right? I guess we just "can't get no satisfaction!"

THE CARES OF THE CHURCH

---

*Never believe that a few caring people can't change
the world. For, indeed, that's all who ever have.*

— Margaret Mead

HE USED ME

When it comes to the cares of the church, Paul, one of the greatest biblical apostles to have lived, said there was nothing like it. Second Corinthians record one of the most descriptive analogies in taking care of the church. Paul gave a brief testimony of all the things he had endured on his journey with Christ. He said:

> Are they servants of Christ?—I speak as if insane—I more so; in far more labors, in far more imprisonments,

beaten times without number, often in danger of death.
Five times I received from the Jews thirty-nine *lashes*.
Three times I was beaten with rods, once I was stoned,
three times I was shipwrecked, a night and a day I have
spent in the deep. *I have been* on frequent journeys, in
dangers from rivers, dangers from robbers, dangers
from *my* countrymen, dangers from the Gentiles,
dangers in the city, dangers in the wilderness, dangers
on the sea, dangers among false brethren; *I have been*
in labor and hardship, through many sleepless nights,
in hunger and thirst, often without food, in   cold
and exposure.

– 2 Corinthians 11:23-27 (NASB)

Can you imagine being stoned? Can you imagine riding on a major cruise line, and the boat begins to break apart? Can you imagine walking in the rugged terrain of the Mississippi woods and being snake-bitten, or the mean streets of a city and being robbed? Paul mentions all the external things he had to endure on top of caring for the church. He said:

Apart from *such* external things, there is the daily pressure on me *of* concern for all the churches. Who is weak
without my being weak? Who is led into sin without my
intense concern?

–2 Corinthians 11:28-29 (NASB)

Paul calls it pressure. Merriam-Webster dictionary defines "pressure" as the continuous physical force exerted on or against an object by something in contact with it. Pastoring is like a consistent Braxton-Hicks contraction. It's a continual force that a Pastor feels in every facet of their lives. The Pastor has the pressure to raise money for the budget. They have the pressure to preach. They also have the pressure of loving the unlovable. The Pastor has the pressure to turn the other cheek and the pressure to perform when there may be hell going on in his or her own life.

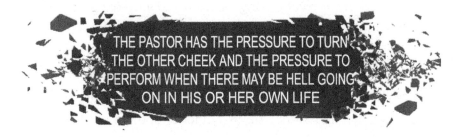

THE PASTOR HAS THE PRESSURE TO TURN THE OTHER CHEEK AND THE PRESSURE TO PERFORM WHEN THERE MAY BE HELL GOING ON IN HIS OR HER OWN LIFE

The Pastor is the instrument used by God to get services to the people. When people have problems, they come to the church. There is an expectancy by people that the Pastor has answers to questions they possess. It doesn't matter if the Pastor doesn't have a law degree. We get legal questions. It doesn't matter whether the Pastor is a licensed practical counselor. He gets clinical questions. It doesn't matter whether the Pastor is a medical doctor. People ask the Pastor medical questions. The expectancy is so high of the church and Pastors that when people are in the crunch financially, they call the church. People often call the church for return in an area they've never invested. Because they expect the man or woman of God is an instrument of God, they can make it happen. They give God credit, and they should, but they often forget that it's the Pastor God is using to bless them. In other words, God is responsible, but He used your Pastor to do it!

PEOPLE OFTEN CALL THE CHURCH FOR RETURN IN AN AREA THEY'VE NEVER INVESTED.

THE LORAX

There are so many life lessons learned while watching cartoons with our kids. Once, I was watching a movie called "The Lorax." There was a memorable quote I'll never forget. He said, "You cannot reap, where you have not sown." The essence of this quote is saying that you don't expect a return in an area you have not planted. We shouldn't go to an ATM and expect a withdrawal if we have not put money in the bank. It's only in the church that people expect a return in an area where they do not contribute. People, in their boldness, believe that the church should be able to assist them. Churches should be able to help those in need. However, the audacity to go a bank and try to withdraw the money you have not placed inside doesn't compute at banks; but the equation is expected to work with the church. It's God's money, they say. It's supposed to be used to help people, they say. They are correct; however, how do you think the money got there? People contribute to the church. Shouldn't the people who provide be the first to receive help if they request it? I'm not asking for a friend. I'm asking for myself.

"YOU CANNOT REAP, WHERE YOU HAVE NOT SOWN."

Recently, I had an epiphany while sitting in worship held by the fastest-growing church in America. This church one November raised nine-million dollars on one Sunday. The church mentioned above averages about fifty-thousand people a Sunday. They are loaded and have a pool of resources. I asked the question during one of the accounting sessions, "Who should the church help?" The chief accountant responded, saying, "the church only has enough money to help its membership." When some apply for benevolence, the church asks for three months' bank statements and that person has to attend financial counseling. I was shocked. All the people in the room begin to comment in disbelief that I helped nonmembers. They said collectively that I should review that policy and make changes immediately. After all, if you give it all the way, the church won't have money to advance the kingdom.

BITTER BENEVOLENCE

We live to give is one of our church mottos. I pondered once, did our church give too much? Yes, churches should provide. We are not banks. We are charities. However, if someone continues to pull out of and never reinvest, the pool of resources will dry up. Usually, people will come to the church as a last resort; however, over the past couple of years, we've seen a trend of people rushing to the church for help and getting angry when they do not qualify.

Years ago, I changed the benevolence process to place it in the hands of those who would look at the emergency assistance package with a critical eye. The group of eagle eyes is composed of Pastors outside of the church, accountants, and other professionals. Since implementing this process, we've let fewer people slip through the cracks of abusing help. We get a request to pay mobile phones, car notes, deposits on apartments, light bills, rent, mortgage, among other things. All of those items do not qualify, but it doesn't keep people from asking. Recently, we had someone who asked for benevolence, and a portion of it was approved. The church paid their past-due light bill to prevent disconnection; and I saw on social media two days later that they were at a high-end resort overseas. Needless to say, I was heated. We were duped by a professional hustler. Usually, it's some applicant who gets bitter by indicating they are a member of the church and the church should help them. They won't serve. They don't give, they just sit on the roll like grandma's oversized Bible on her prized coffee table. With this particular incident, I became angry. The church had been burned. I thought, how could someone abuse the system set to help them? As a result, the committee selected to conduct reviews does so with a more careful eye.

WHEN IT COMES TO BENEVOLENCE, PEOPLE HAVE SHORT MEMORIES.

When it comes to benevolence, people have short memories. I assisted this one guy who had just gotten back from prison. I pitched in to help him personally by giving him about seven suits and men's blazers. We knew that it was going to take a little bit to get him on his feet. After a while, we had to realize that he didn't want help. He wanted to create a habit through handouts. In ministry, we have to be consistent in helping people who want to help themselves. Consistently throughout scripture, we see people needing support. People wanted to be whole or healed. It was their desire to get cured that yielded help from Jesus. We assisted this man by even paying for a week at his extended-stay hotel after being evicted by his family. Days later, we got a call from some of the family members asking why the church didn't help him. He had told his family that he had never received assistance from the church. I guess ministry assistance has a short memory. There are times we have assisted people in their worst times. The same individuals would go on social media and tell people otherwise.

ONE-STOP SHOP

The shock would vibrate through people if they only knew the full range of responsibilities of Pastors. People expect their Pastors to be superheroes. We're not superheroes, we are Clark Kents with God-supernatural wisdom. One of the toughest events Pastors have to witness is the incarceration of one of their members. We walk them through the indictments, through the court proceeding, and ultimately sentencing. We see people get years for their crimes even after praying that God would show them mercy. We're in a situation where we can't offer answers, only shoulders to cry upon and warm voices to console their kids. Once there was a lady who was involved in an accident involving alcohol. Although the case was complicated, it was hard to see a good person get punished for one wrong decision. Her lawyer indicated that she would get about three years plus probation, so that's what we were expecting at best. Me and one of my assistants in ministry sat in court waiting for the judge to render her decision. We were waiting for what was promised. The judge chastised her and said, "I'm giving you twenty years and suspending five." I was broken for days, if not weeks. It felt as if my daughter was just given that time. That day, a part of me felt incarcerated. Time after time, I've appeared in court for members. The public will never see the "not so glorious" duties a Pastor has to partake.

WE'RE NOT SUPERHEROES, WE ARE CLARK KENTS WITH GOD-SUPERNATURAL WISDOM.

As a Pastor, I'm often asked legal questions and asked to guide people through the legal process. Years ago, I spent a significant amount of time working in a defense firm. I was on my way to law school. I handled over six-thousand cases and did thousands of trial charts, sifted through thousands of depositions, and prepared even more motions for summary judgments than the average lawyer. As a result, I do have some experience in this field, but the notion that people feel comfortable to ask their Pastor legal questions adds to the list of duties and responsibilities for the shepherd. I've lead people through worker's comp, sexual harassment cases, and other lawsuits by pointing them in the direction to get help. As Pastors, we have to be careful about how we advise. If you're not certified to counsel, you give advisement according to the scripture only. We should only suggest and allow the person to choose based on the options available. One of the frivolities of immaturity is attempting to be God in someone's life. *We are guides, not gods.*

IF YOU'RE NOT CERTIFIED TO COUNSEL,
YOU GIVE ADVISEMENT ACCORDING
TO THE SCRIPTURE ONLY.

Over the years, I've guided dozens of people, which ultimately led to victories in the jurisprudence system. The observation I've made in every instance is that those individuals either no longer attend regularly or left the church. Since we're talking about the pain of Pastors, let's be candid. Of the millions awarded to individuals I've advised, neither my church nor I have ever received a dime. We are often the Pastor of the nine ungrateful lepers. No, we are not entitled to anything, and that's not why we help; but the consideration of saying thanks for your help should be a norm.

I'M HERE

Pastors are called upon for the hatching, matching, and dispatching of congregants and those involved. When a baby is born, we dedicate the baby to the Lord. When someone wants to tie the knot, we give them classes and guide them along on their important day. These are indeed joyous moments. However, we are called to dispatch members of the church more than to their dedication and nuptials. Dying can be one of the most difficult times in a person's life. They call their Pastor because we are equipped. Many Pastors are equipped with wisdom to guide people through the vicissitudes of life. The words we say are not always what people need. They need our presence. They need our hearts. Sometimes they simply need to look into our eyes and get the sense that everything will be okay. As death takes a toll on the people, it also takes a toll on the Pastor. To see people hurting in such an abysmal fashion, takes a toll on us mentally, emotionally, and even spiritually. Once again, most people forget that as we are helping them "do life," we too are experiencing life. Let talk about it!

MOST PEOPLE FORGET THAT AS WE ARE HELPING THEM "DO LIFE," WE TOO ARE EXPERIENCING LIFE.

WE TOO

Obviously, those reading this book immediately thought about the "Me Too" movement when they saw the heading. I am by no means attempting to diminish the velocity of movement, I'm using it as a play on words that "we too" experience the many woes of life. We spend countless hours being there for members during the death of their loved ones.

I've experienced the lack of empathy for what Pastors go through years ago. While I was a Pastor, my grandmother passed. Understand, my grandmother was my rock. She raised me a large portion of my life. She is the one who kept me in church. She played for five different Baptist churches throughout Vicksburg, Mississippi. I remember right before service started, I would sing "Go Tell It on the Mountain" at King David #1. Back then, the churches would have numbers assigned when the church divided. Instead of coming up with a new name, they would keep the name and just order the number nominally. She was the strongest woman I knew. At the time she passed away, my church was inclining rapidly. I had at least a thousand members. Ask me how many appeared at the funeral. I had enough members alone to fill up that sanctuary twice. I could count on both hands how many came to show their support. Unfortunately, there is an unwritten expectation that the Pastor doesn't need help. The Pastor doesn't need money. The Pastor doesn't need space. We need the same things the parishioner needs. I believe every Pastor needs a Pastor. We need information, we need support, we need money to take care of our families, and we need consoling during times of grief. I didn't hold it against the folks I lead. It was at this time that I realized that pain associated with pastoring. We are expected to heal fast and get over it while giving others get the time they need. I deal with this notion in greater depth later in the book.

THERE IS AN UNWRITTEN EXPECTATION THAT THE PASTOR DOESN'T NEED HELP.

THE PRESSURE TO PREACH

EACH TIME A PASTOR STANDS AT THAT MIC, PEOPLE EXPECT THE FIRE TO COME FROM HEAVEN.

I have the precious privilege to cover Pastors across the country. One of the hardest tasks that many of them complain about is the difficulty in constructing messages. On average, it takes about eight hours to build a well-developed message. Each time a Pastor stands at that mic, people expect the fire to come from heaven. People drive from far and wide, sometimes using their last bit of gas on their only day off, to come to hear something to change their life. Many times, we have visitors laced throughout the sanctuary, and it feels like we're on trial every time we touch the mic. The pressure to preach is real. Imagine writing an eight-page paper twice weekly, and it has to be interesting enough to not put the listeners to sleep. People who have been in church a while have heard the same stories over and over. Dr. Vernon, writer of *Help! My Pastor Is Under Pressure*, explains this notion by writing, "no matter how many times he preaches on Daniel and the Lion Den, he still comes out alive in the end. Moses' bush is still burning, and after learning his lesson, the Prodigal Son comes back home chill, and his brother is still sulking and side-eyeing him." How many times can we preach the same stories and interest people? As a result, we have to study Greek and Hebrew. We have to read material on the subjects or texts to help give fresh insight to the listeners. The process can be laborious, and if the Pastor has one off-day, members and supporters will leave saying that they no longer have "the edge."

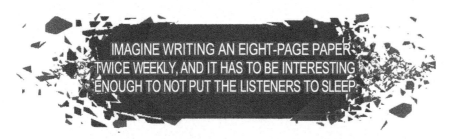

IMAGINE WRITING AN EIGHT-PAGE PAPER TWICE WEEKLY, AND IT HAS TO BE INTERESTING ENOUGH TO NOT PUT THE LISTENERS TO SLEEP.

CREATIVITY

In the twenty-first century, people learn differently. Our modern classrooms are filled with white-boards, screens, and other exciting technology. As a consequence of this shift to a technologically advanced generation, churches are forced to tap into the technology to perk the interest of the listeners. The dilemma is the more technology to which a person is exposed, the shorter the attention span. Pastors have the pressure to infuse creativity in their messages to accentuate points because the brains of the listeners receive differently. Recently, I had a tug-o-war in the middle of the service to drive home the struggle of the flesh and the spirit. The point went over well, but I had to set it up so that people could understand. I had to buy supplies. I had to incorporate the analogy into the overall theme of what I was preaching. Creativity can be an arduous process. Sometimes, it takes teams to keep fresh ideas flowing.

EVERY PASTOR NEEDS TO GET AWAY AND THINK.

For this reason, every Pastor needs to get away and think. When a Pastor doesn't take breaks, fatigue will quell their creativity. If I stop thinking, many of those I pastor will stop spiritually feasting. It is vitally important for every Pastor to have seasons of filling after seasons of pouring.

IT IS VITALLY IMPORTANT FOR EVERY PASTOR TO HAVE SEASONS OF FILLING AFTER SEASONS OF POURING.

BEFORE I BREAK SOMETHING

In the fourteenth chapter of Mathew, Jesus went away to pray. Additionally, we find throughout the text that Jesus got away to rest. He left the mundane work of the ministry to the disciples, and he slept. Nowhere in the text indicates that Jesus had trouble sleeping. He received all of his sleep no matter what was going on. Jesus set the

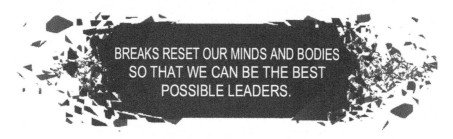

BREAKS RESET OUR MINDS AND BODIES SO THAT WE CAN BE THE BEST POSSIBLE LEADERS.

model. As a leader, you have to break away from the crowd. We have to take sabbaticals, vacations, mini-excursions, or whatever to keep our sanity. Breaks reset our minds and bodies so that we can be the best possible leaders. The dilemma is that members many times don't want us to take breaks. I've had people ride by the church and look for my vehicle. If they don't see it, they keep driving. Some have had the nerve to send me messages stating, "You've been gone two Sundays." Catching me out of my humility, I would sometimes reply, "You took off half the year, and I haven't said anything." Hey, we all get in the flesh and sometimes, but this and illustrated example how many parishioners do not consider the health and the wellbeing of the pastor. It's important, as pastors, that we are proactive in maintaining good mental health by taking regular breaks.

As a consequence, many Pastors do not announce their absence, because members will stay home, offerings will be lower, and the services may not have the same flair as if the Pastor was there. This is not always my testimony. We have matured to the point where I can leave, and people still join, receive Jesus, and the offering remains unscathed. However, this is the testimony of many Pastors across the country. In an attempt to meet budget numbers and not kill momentum, they push through breaks and ultimately end up breaking their marriage, social life, ministry influence, or one of the member's hearts. The pressure to be present is real for the majority of the Pastors in America because members do not want to grow up, and they become handicapped by the Pastor's absence.

HOME ALONE

When I was a youth, there were a series of movies entitled "Home Alone." The star of the film was Macaulay Culkin. The thematic thrust of the movies was about a young boy inadvertently left at home alone by his parents as they vacationed. In their absence, criminals attempted to rob the house, but the young star's creative ingenuity prevented them from successfully stealing anything. Notice as you reminisce upon this classic film that the crooks never attempted to come through the front door. They tried windows, chimneys, basements, and so on. Many Pastors feel they can't take breaks because, in their absence, the grievous wolves will enter with an attempt to highjack the congregation and rob the flock of peace and process. Numerous examples I remember coming up as a young minister. One Pastor left, and when he came back, his senior assistant changed the name of the church along with the locks. Like an airplane highjacked, it appeared to have been a well-planned and thought-out process. As Pastors, we have to be ever so careful who we leave in the care of the flock. As a result, many Pastors call ministers from the outside to preach while absent from their responsibilities, because with whomever you share the platform, you give influence. A crafty senior assistant or charismatic minister can take one-third of the congregation. Sounds familiar?

There are so many pressures that derive from pastoring. Scripture talks about the grievous wolves from the outside, but it's the ones on the inside that can hurt you more. The ones on the inside know your Achilles heel and sometimes will use your weakness against you. As Pastors, we have to be careful who we pull into our inner circle. Additionally, those who travel abundantly must have systems in place that will guard against those coming through the back door.

THE PRESSURE FOR PERFECTION

Webster defines perfection as the quality or state of being perfect. It is an exemplification of supreme excellence and an unsurpassable degree of accuracy. No person can meet the qualification of that definition. I personally cannot. The person reading this book will fall short of this definition as well. However, people looking in from the outside may not verbalize or voice their opinion that they want their Pastor perfect, but their actions reflect otherwise. Before I proceed, let me say that when you're called to public service of any form, you're expected to maintain a certain level of integrity, standard, and class. I am by no means excusing the behaviors of those in the public light. Whether a politician, teacher, officer, or preacher, we should live above the fray. I would advise that no one assume those positions until their character matches the position.

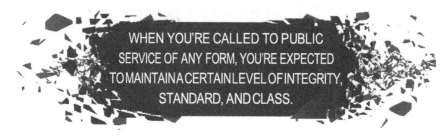

WHEN YOU'RE CALLED TO PUBLIC SERVICE OF ANY FORM, YOU'RE EXPECTED TO MAINTAIN A CERTAIN LEVEL OF INTEGRITY, STANDARD, AND CLASS.

Additionally, it's possible to start on a particular path and lose your focus. Like the disciple, Peter, who took steps to do what no other man had done, stepped out on the water. He was successful for a while until he took his eyes off the one who sustained his success. It is possible to have a vision, have focus, have a drive, have integrity, but lose it amid a storm. We have to remember everyone is susceptible to something. We each us must put on our pants a leg at a time. Each is subject to like passions, and no one is above failure. What I am articulating is that parishioners do not extend the same grace of God that they would expect. People hold those in the public eye to a standard they cannot keep themselves. On any given week, someone will come into my office or grace one of my social media inboxes confessing unruly behaviors. People have acknowledged orgies, drug binges, domestic abuse, and much more vile stuff I cannot repeat. Many of these practices are not even acceptable among the immoral. We are to keep a straight face and minister to them the best way possible. As a Pastor, we live in the basement of other people's secrets. We must administer the words of His grace and let people know that there is life after failure. No one reading this text would disagree with that assessment. Galatians says if one of your brothers falls into sin, help restore them. The scripture should apply to every person who falls into sin regardless of that title. However, that scripture doesn't always apply to Pastors.

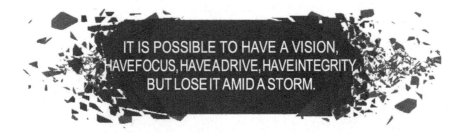

IT IS POSSIBLE TO HAVE A VISION, HAVE FOCUS, HAVE A DRIVE, HAVE INTEGRITY, BUT LOSE IT AMID A STORM.

Each year, Pastors fall into strange behavior unbecoming of their calling. Some openly admit it, while others are exposed. Whatever the source of outing Pastors may be, the standard applied to parishioners is not the same as that applied to Pastors. The chatters of "I can't believe they did that" often spread through the community like a rare strain of influenza. The whispers cast doubts on the fallen Pastors' calling, and people flee like bullets riddling an enclosed room. Many Pastors never recover; yet grace shouldn't only apply to sheep. The shepherd at all times needs the same grace extended to others, but it is a rarity. As a result, Pastors have to create a veneer that they are near perfect to appease people who want perfection. Many of us have become accustomed to openly talking about our struggle to remind people that we are just like you but called to speak to you. So, to those reading this, understand that your Pastor is human. They, like you, have something tailored to their weakness that, at any given time, can draw them from walking on water and cause them to sink in that sunken place.

PEOPLE HOLD THOSE IN THE PUBLIC EYE TO A STANDARD THEY CANNOT KEEP THEMSELVES.

THE PRESSURE TO RAISE MONEY

For years there have been "taboo" topics churches avoided addressing. Some of these topics, including domestic violence, sex, homosexuality, and of course, money! Our society is built up as a medium of exchange. That medium of exchange is controlled by the U.S. Mint and places a value on the paper, nickel, and copper. We exchange goods and services for these dollars. Our society is built upon this notion. We can't survive without it. Why is it a strange notion that churches need money to survive as well? We need cash for necessary operating expenses such as light bills, mortgages, and staffing. We need money to be able to bless others in their time of need.

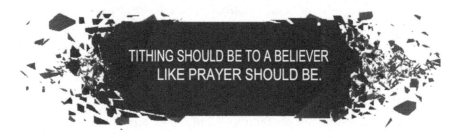

TITHING SHOULD BE TO A BELIEVER
LIKE PRAYER SHOULD BE.

Additionally, many churches like the one I pastor engage in philanthropic endeavors throughout the community. We need money! As a result, Pastors are pressured like CEOs many times to meet specific budget indicators to ensure the needs are met through the church.

Pastors wouldn't have to experience this pressure if members did their part. Tithing is your reasonable service. Tithing is the first oracle and fundamental principle of Christianity. Tithing should be to a believer like prayer should be. People say they believe in the ministry and the church and as a result, a Pastor shouldn't have to twist arms to get people to donate. There are churches all over the country operating in the red, and it's because people who claim to support the church don't support the church. Even while this book is being published, we're in the middle of a Pandemic. The crisis revealed that many churches are living offering to offering. Some people claim to believe in God, but not his command to give. Not all who are reading this book are Christians, but believers should understand that what you hold is your seed, but whatever you release is the beginning of your harvest. Most people eat their seed and end up in lack because they don't replant. If everyone in church performed their God-commanded duty, the communities would not lack.

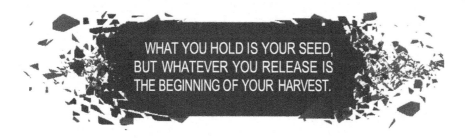

WHAT YOU HOLD IS YOUR SEED, BUT WHATEVER YOU RELEASE IS THE BEGINNING OF YOUR HARVEST.

The pressure to raise money for special projects is even harder. I'm in one of the poorest states in America but one of the most charitable. Most people have adopted the philosophy that they'll support it after it's done. Well, that's great, but we need support to get there. Before your minds wander in the abyss, some have misused the gifts of givers for personal gain. However, corporations across America have misused our data and dollars. We still bank at Wells Fargo, we always utilize Equifax, and always go to black Friday at Wal-Mart. It's only when it comes to the isolated incidents at church that we poison the well and overgeneralize that ALL churches must engage in financial malfeasance. Most churches have internal controls that disallow frivolous spending and ensure proper management according to the IRS code. The pressure to raise money is heightened, knowing that many people have reservations about giving to churches regardless of the track record. Some hold the belief that the Pastor will buy a fancy car and big house with their money, when the majority of the Pastors in the United States don't receive a salary, stipend, vacation, or any other gift from the church.

Furthermore, if a Pastor wants to buy fancy cars or a lovely house, they can do so with their salary. Whatever salary they receive, they have the liberty to purchase what they want, just like you do. It's an underlying issue that people want their Pastor to live well, just not better than them.

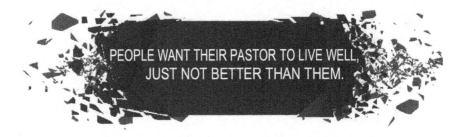

PEOPLE WANT THEIR PASTOR TO LIVE WELL, JUST NOT BETTER THAN THEM.

Caring for the church can be a taxing responsibility. Like a doctor who deals with the sick, Pastors deals with emotional and spiritually sick people. They say and do stuff that's offensive and hurtful. It's part of the job description. Caring for the church is a calling. One has to be equipped by God to handle the environment. The environment can be toxic, but if one is adequately prepared, they can work with anthrax. Sadly, many Pastors, including some who are reading this book, weren't equipped for the pain they endured in the line of duty. Consequently, we have injured soldiers trying to continue the work of the ministry while stepping over the bodies of shepherds who didn't survive the vicious bites of the sheep they lead.

NEW LEVEL, NEW DEVIL

Love is the only weapon I have, I will defend
with love, I will attack with respect.

— Amit Kalantri

SLANDER

I remember while in college riding the down the street in Greenville, Mississippi, in my fully loaded Chevy Impala. Out of nowhere, a brick penetrated my windshield. I remember the shock that caused my heart to sink into a dismal rhythm as if it was entering a cardiac arrest. I pulled over to the side of the road to calm my shaken nerves before gathering myself to call the police. To this day, I don't know who threw the brick or whether it was an unintentional projectile launched by one of the many semi-trucks that frequented that street. No matter the cause, I was shocked. Can you imagine minding your business and suddenly something shocking happens? I remember like it was yesterday. I was at a resort in Miramar, Florida when my Facebook inbox began to buzz. The first person was a praise team member, who simply said, "Some guy on Facebook Live is talking about you." In the line of Pastoring, being talked about isn't anything strange. People can sit right in the sanctuary Sunday after Sunday and immediately following service, they serve themselves roasted Pastor for brunch and fried clergy for dinner. One of the most confusing and baffling phenomena is how someone can go to a church they don't like and sit under a Pastor they don't respect. This attack was different. It proved to be one that would take my ministry on a journey further than I would have liked to go.

An ex-convict and failed Pastor in my city was trying to build a platform. He had attacked many politicians, city officials, and others who had influence. He had exposed their addresses, making their safety a genuine concern. He had gone down a whole list of people concocting stories of them having infectious diseases, affairs, stealing from their employers, and a host of other vicious lies hurled with the intent to damage their reputation. Guess who was next? Right! Me.

KEEPING MY NOSE CLEAN

I have not had an inkling of scandal. My name was cleaner than a newborn baby's bottom. I prided myself on staying out of a mess, treating people right, and blessed the community. The worst thing that people could say about me is that I was arrogant. What they didn't know was that was my defense mechanism to keep people from getting too close to me and especially ladies from attempting to flirt with me. I'll take arrogant over other things any day! One of my mentors told me early in ministry before affirming me as a minister, "Roderick, keep your nose clean." It was until years later I really understood the context of that statement. He meant, stay out of trouble. Don't let your name keep intertwined in a mess. Protect your name. I did just that. I avoided political endorsements, side chicks, financial malfeasance, and many of the pitfalls that Pastors can find themselves trapped on the journey towards Christ. Oddly, seven years into my ministry, it seemed that God wanted to take me to another level of prayer. Every attack is to align you to another level of consecration. For those reading this body of work, keep your nose clean. Those words proved to be ones that saved my ministry and my life.

EVERY ATTACK IS TO ALIGN YOU TO ANOTHER LEVEL OF CONSECRATION.

OPPORTUNISTIC

The ex-convict opportunist launched a visceral attack to see how it would go. He noticed that over ten-thousand people viewed his video. It was his most massive Facebook Live to date. People wanted to see what this guy had on the local Pastor who had kept his nose clean. I was like the local Robin Hood. We fed the poor, we gave out free gas to random motorists, we formed backpack drives that assisted thousands. During the City of Jackson water crisis, we gave out over twenty tons of water to whosoever needed it. We didn't care whether they were black, white, blue, or yellow. It didn't matter what neighborhood they came from, we helped everyone. I had done nothing but good, and for the first time, an amalgamation of people logged on to hear something terrible. The opportunistic guy knew he had hit a gold mine. His angle was simple. A young lady he found out went to our church was in the news for something that allegedly happened at a local university. He found out this young lady went to my church. Keep in mind, when you have thousands on membership roll and half of that attending each Sunday, it's impossible to know everyone who graces the threshold of your doors. He needed the attention and wanted to make a connection so bad he reached for an opportunity—like opportunistic people do.

CAN'T EAT AT EVERYBODY'S HOUSE

I remember growing up, my mother would tell me, "You can't eat at everybody's house." The reason is that people weren't always clean. Some people had decent food, but the environment it was prepared in was not clean. Grandma used to go to the extent of saying explicitly, don't eat anybody's spaghetti and anyone's chitterlings. These items were Southern dishes, but everyone didn't know how to prepare them, and everyone definitely didn't clean chitterlings as thoroughly as she did. This taught me to always consider the source. No matter how good a cook they were, if roaches, grease, and grit existed in the environment, don't eat at their house. I know you're asking what this has to do with anything. You have to consider the source. The convict and the opportunistic person who attacked me was just recently released from prison. His past was more checkered than a chessboard. He had been in and out of jail since he was fourteen. His felony charges included embezzling money from a church. Go figure! Later, the Ridgeland DA stated, "His rap sheet is as long as the Dead Sea scroll." The guy was bad news, yet he was serving news to a collective audience of thousands. He served what he called "tea." It was heart-wrenching that many citizens were eating from a dirty plate.

WEE WEE IN THE WATER

I remember hearing this story of three guys who went to confession at a Catholic Church. The first guy entered to converse with the priest and told the priest he was there to confess. He confessed that he had cheated on his wife. The priest gave him his spill and told him to drink from the holy water. The second guy entered admitting that he had cheated on his taxes. The priest echoed the same sentiments by giving him instructions and told him to take two drinks from the holy water. The third guy came in, and the priest asked him what did he want to confess. He said, "Father, I urinated in the holy water." Take the time to laugh a little. You see where I'm going with it. When someone "wee wees" in the water, it impacts all those who come after them. The source had become contaminated. Slander, in a profession like pastoring, contaminates its victims and casts reservations on the person's reputation, character, and integrity. It doesn't matter if the information is factual. The only thing a shallow public sector needs to hear is that it was said. Imagine the hundreds who have been exonerated from the allegations that the public later found weren't real. The damage had been done. Although this guy said in many of the videos he had created, "I don't have anything on Pastor Rich," the people wanted to pool me with others and use it as a justification to not believe in the institution of the church.

Friedrich Nietzsche said, "It is easier to cope with a bad conscience than a bad reputation." It's easy to declare that you don't care about other people's opinions, but we must live in a community where we depend on the views of others. We can't neglect the fact that other people should matter. Ideas are so healthy that companies such as Trip Advisor and Yelp have built profitable companies by utilizing community opinions. These opinions can drive or garner people to your entity. Robert Greene, the writer of *The 48 Laws of Power*, writes of the difficulty of defending slander. P.T. Barnum, of the famed Barnum and Bailey Circus, used this visceral weapon against his competition to bring himself notoriety and to bring his competitors to their demise. Greene writes:

> Barnum used two different tactics to ruin Peale's repu-
> tation. The first was simple: He sowed doubts about the
> museum's stability and solvency. Doubt is a powerful
> weapon: Once you let it out of the bag with insidious
> rumors, your opponents are in a horrible dilemma.
>
> On the one hand, they can deny the rumors, even prove
> that you have slandered them. But a layer of suspicion
> will remain: Why are they defending themselves so
> desperately? Maybe the rumor has some truth to it? If,
> on the other hand, they take the high road and ignore
> you, the doubts, unrefuted, will be even stronger. If
> done correctly, the sowing of rumors can so infuriate
> and unsettle your rivals that in defending themselves,
> they will make numerous mistakes. This is the perfect
> weapon for those who have no reputation of their own
> to work from.

It can take years to recover from slander, just as with P.T. Barnum's victims. One of his significant competitors lost money, reputation, and public appeal for his business. The notion of slander works just as strong today as it did in Barnum's day. As a Pastor, our profession is laced and intertwined in one's ability to live what they are preaching. No one is perfect by any means, but the public expects the Pastor to live above the fray and above reproach. Paul declared in 1 Timothy 3:2 that the leader or overseer must be above reproach. Slander is the tool that will sink any proven leader to the depths of the sea regardless of how fruitful they've previously been portrayed.

DAMAGE CONTROL

I was inadequately prepared for an attack of this magnitude. I consulted a public relations firm to assess the damage and to give me a strategy on how to handle an attack of this nature. It was determined that I didn't need to say anything publicly. I was instructed not to even make a statement to the church. The silence was one of the hardest things I've ever had to do to-date. I'm a talker. I wanted to defend myself. I was the clap-back king! I desired to get online and roast the guy who slandered me. It was during these times that I understood the scripture that said Jesus didn't say a mumbling word. I took the lashes. I took the beating across social media.

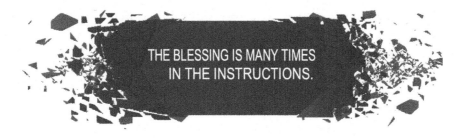

THE BLESSING IS MANY TIMES IN THE INSTRUCTIONS.

My membership knew that I was vocal about everything, but I was silent about this. Parishioners knew I would fight back, because I am a fighter. It's not that I didn't want to say anything. I was following instructions. The blessing is many times in the instructions. My silence obviously was interpreted as guilt. However, most of those who criticized my silence had never been in the spotlight. The picture was larger than the small minds that gossiped about it. I had a platform. He didn't. His aim was to profit from what God had built. When you become a person of influence, people will attack you to draw likes to their site. His aim was to tear me down with an effort to lift himself up. His motive was purely evil because he was someone I've never met. I've never run across him. I told myself, I was just another local person on his list who had notoriety. I was simply next in line. His rants against me were different, though. They seemed highly personal from a person whom I've never met. Later, we found one of the reasons for his malicious attacks. While he was in prison, his wife and family joined my church. I was the man feeding his family while he was paying restitution for his constant bad decisions. However, the damage had been done.

All one must do is cast doubt on a Pastor's name. It doesn't matter if it's true. Mere allegations have damaged hundreds of Pastors and marred what took years to build. Yes, my integrity stood the test of time, but now I was blemished. Some Pastors go to the extreme in prevented this type of damage. They're never seen in public. They don't engage on social media. They're obsessive. I'm an extrovert, and I love people. I couldn't go that route. Also, African American Pastors must do more than our Caucasian brothers. They don't have to have social media accounts. They don't have to engage. They can have walls up between them and the membership, which creates buffers of contact. We, as African American Pastors, must be accessible. It's not fair, but it's life in American Christendom.

BARKING UP THE WRONG TREE

Things had been quiet for about a month or so. My name was occasionally mentioned. I wasn't bothered, because I knew I had handled matters right. I weathered the storm. One night I decided to go work out with one of my members. He's a buff guy who looked like he could lift the back end of the train. With someone like that working out with me, I was sure to tone my flab. As we were in the gym posting video, I get a notification saying, "Get the fuck out of my gym." Another one said, "Don't bring your shit around here." Let me back up so you can know the person who's writing this book a little better. I wasn't always in church. I ran the streets with some pretty tough people. When you subscribe to the church, your "old man" is supposed to be dead. Death is often proverbial. I knew exactly where he lived, and even when I deliver messages, he has a tendency to show his head. The day this guy decided to bully me in my place of peace, the old man was with me. I was about to blast this fellow, and he had no idea of who I used to be. We were at this prominent gym and I decided to approach him. I'll never forget the fear on his face. First, he was surely shocked that I was of a muscular stature. I was of larger size than he probably imagined. In fact, I had a larger frame than him and I was more fit. I remember him stammering like a bully who finally got confronted. I told him, "You don't know who I am." I was fed up. He was afraid to come from behind the desk. He knew that day, I wasn't Pastor nobody. I was Roderick Richardson and I was about to put my foot in his you know what. I heard a calming voice from one of my members, "Pastor, let's go." I left that night hotter than a habanero pepper! That day, I met my slanderer face to face. For the first time, I realized he was a coward and keyboard gangster-like many others who hide behind electronics.

THREAT

It's not uncommon for a Pastor to get death threats. Some of the most prominent Pastors receive threats at least once a month. For this reason, many churches employ volunteer and full-time security. Over the years, people have shot Pastors and stabbed First Ladies for various reasons. Sometimes these threats come because of teaching that changes their mate's lifestyle. I've had calls from guys saying, "You're the guy that told my woman to stop sleeping with me." Not exactly. We teach not having sex before marriage. So, if their mate gravitates towards that teaching, it will change the environment of that household. As a result, we're left to deal with disgruntled people, especially men. That night when I left the gym, the keyboard gangster did what he does best. He went online and acted hard. He threatened to come by my church the following Sunday. He said he and his goons were going to show up to disrupt services. In that video, he threatened to come after my family and me no matter where he saw me. He threatened me with a Smith & Wesson. He had access to this company's database. This is how he knew I was in the gym. On that video, he called out an address that was only listed on that account. I hadn't used that address on anything. His revealing that address was an indication that this guy had my personal information. What he did that night changed everything! To date, I'm not sure what was revealed in that account. I had a credit card on file, personal numbers, old addresses, and much more. Over the next couple of weeks,

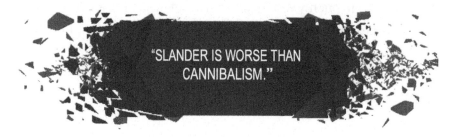

"SLANDER IS WORSE THAN CANNIBALISM."

he went on a rampage slandering me. I was everything from gay to loving all the ladies. Anything he could think of, I was called. He leveled more threats. He revealed old addresses that were in the gym's system. He created stories like a novel writer. The hurting element was that people listened. People listened as he launched fallacious attacks on me, my church, those close to me, and my family. John Chrysostom said, "Slander is worse than cannibalism." The city had a feast. People are always looking for negative things to say about the church to excuse their illicit behavior. I was the meal of the month, and the city feasted on what he called "tea." It didn't matter that none of what this complete stranger was saying was right; it was something negative and there was a parasitic atmosphere in my city. He was Wendy Williams and the town was his audience.

COLLATERAL DAMAGE

The slander had grown out of control. People wanted me to respond, but I was under advisement. They didn't know the counsel I received. I was following instructions. The talk became so pervasive that I received questions everywhere I went. People close to me started to feel the impact of the conversation. I had people who had been with me day one, leave the church. On top of slander, I had people to leave, who swore loyalty to us. The kitchen was hot. There is an abundance of lessons I learned during this time. People will ride with you as long as things are good. The test of loyalty is not when it's okay, but when it's tough. It was tough times. I saw an attendance decrease. I saw the offering dwindle. I felt like I was on an island all by myself. What was interesting is that not one Pastor I had aligned with in the city said anything. The guy admitted it was all a lie, but it was entertaining. It wasn't entertaining for those who have been on the other end of slander. I understand that my people hurt as I did. I can't tell you the countless individuals who approached me, saying, "We can take care of him, Pastor." My flesh wanted to say, "Yeah, blow his house up or something," but I settled for the Christian response. I told them we're Christians and we do not handle business like the streets. The truth is I was still trying to recover from the barrage of social media bullets. I had spun into a deep depression. It felt like I'd been to Desert Storm and just returned to the states attempting to process what I saw. I couldn't trust anyone. I become paranoid, wondering what did people believe? I was contemplating breaking protocol with my public relations firm because holding the truth in was like holding your breath for minutes at a time. I was miserable.

While waddling in my misery, I was still called upon to preach, oversee financials, assist with the marketing, manage staff, and spiritually advise others. The truth is that this is the plight of many Pastors, even ones reading this book. The only strong element in my life was my marriage, but Pastors' marriages are falling away while trying to keep themselves and the church together. The travesty is that many are the silence of the lambs. They quietly implode while smiling in front of their congregations. I'll address the fallen soldiers in a later chapter. I was dying, but required to give life to others. I was leading and bleeding. I was collateral damage for the hatred someone had for the church at large yet I was still charged with Pastoring with a smile.

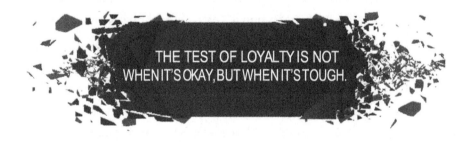

THE TEST OF LOYALTY IS NOT WHEN IT'S OKAY, BUT WHEN IT'S TOUGH.

CIVILITY

I've always prided myself on practicing what I preach. I don't always hit the mark, because I am still human. For the most part, I walk in a grace that prevents me from staying in sin. I've learned during this process that you don't know what you would do and how you would handle something until you're in the actual situation. The night of the confrontation at the gym, the guy went too far. I decided to treat things civilly. I filed charges in my county, and the district attorney immediately took up the case. He woke the judge in the wee hours of the morning to sign the warrant. What's interesting is one night while he was talking about me, they came to his house and arrested him while on Facebook Live. How ironic! The platform that he used to slander people was the one used to embarrass him. It was after the arrest that we discovered how extensive his arrest record was. His criminal behavior spanned several decades. I was just another victim in a crime of opportunity. The local DA sent the case to the grand jury, and he was indicted on the threats he leveled against me. Months later he went to trial, the jury of his peers convicted him, and he was sentenced eight years to the Mississippi Department of Corrections. Talk about vindication!

VINDICATION

I remember leaving the sentencing with a smile on my face. I wanted to tell the world! It wouldn't take long for news to spread that an internet assault was prosecuted, and someone received years in the state penitentiary for social media slander. It was the first time in the State of Mississippi that this law was used in a trial and successfully gained a sentence. My phone was buzzing as if every call center in the country shared my credentials and was eager to give me a call. I received calls from other Pastors, politicians, and parishioners. I received text messages and inboxes from others. People made posts about it, and shock spread to the uttermost parts of Mississippi and a few connecting states. People knew now why I didn't say a mumbling word. On top of the criminal case, I decided to take civil litigation against him and everyone connected. I may never receive a dime from him, but he'll remember me for the rest of his life. Some overzealous and sacrilegious saints will surely say, why are you gloating in someone else's downfall? Where is the grace for the person who victimized you? Grace is available from the repentant heart. Even as I write this book, the assailant continues to post about me and others from prison.

Later, we found out that the appellate courts overturned the conviction because the district attorney's office filed the wrong charge. I had the option to refile under Mississippi's Cyberstalking law, but I decided to give him some grace. I knew from that point, the whole ordeal caused me to grow as a person and a pastor. I've forgiven him. As a result, the time he spent behind bars will be a reminder that he barked up the wrong tree!

WHAT DOESN'T COME OUT IN THE WASH

While conversing with Bishop Joseph Walker III, the Presiding Bishop of Full Gospel, he gave me wisdom on the wash. Years ago, he went through a severe challenge with slander. People had come forth levying unsubstantiated allegations. He said while going through this challenge, he lost five-hundred members. When the news reported that he was cleared, twenty-five hundred joined. The Bishop told me that "a lie will fly, but will not stand, because it has no legs." He also said things will happen, especially early in your ministry, to wash it. Could what I was going through be washing? It's throwing the "Jonahs" off the boat. In the early church, there was a pervasive example of persecution. The martyrs were boiled alive, crucified, and stoned among other heinous acts of torture.

"A LIE WILL FLY, BUT WILL NOT STAND, BECAUSE IT HAS NO LEGS."

Before the Edict of Milan, there was an open season on believers. When I begin to put things in perspective, what is it that we go through now as believers? Internet assaults? Members leaving? Betrayal? These types of events present opportunities to find out what's in the hearts of those who say they love their leadership. God will allow small events to happen to "wash" your ministry. Allow it! The Pastor needs someone who will celebrate their highs and uplift them when they are low. We need people who when allowed the opportunity to be disloyal, won't jump off the boat—they will grab a sword and protect its assets.

NEW LEVELS, NEW DEVILS

I recently had a scare with death. When a doctor says, "you were sick," there should be a genuine concern. During an extended celebration of my wife's fortieth birthday, we decided to go to the mountains of Colorado. We were going to scratch some stuff off our bucket list. We decided we're going skiing and snowmobiling. Unbeknownst to us, we were going to one of the highest points in Colorado. After landing, grabbing our bags and rent-a-car, we were on our way! As soon as we hit the highway, snow and ice bombarded us like bomb cyclones. Our windshield wipers froze, and I occasionally had to stick my hand out of the window to clear the ice. The expected trip was scheduled to take about two hours and fifteen minutes, but it took many hours instead. As we climbed the mountains to get to our cabin, we saw people sliding off the road, getting stuck on the highway, and even sliding backward. I couldn't help but think that going to new levels can often bring unexpected delays. Sometimes we climb the proverbial ladder of our careers, ministry, or relationships; sometimes the conditions are not conducive to reaching our destination in the planned time. We can expect detours of sickness, poor planning, and even attacks. After seven hours of grueling delays, we arrived at our destination. I grabbed my bags and walked into my cabin. Immediately I was short of breath. I thought I was in pretty good shape. I asked the others if they were experiencing shortness of breath. Many of them said they were, but my gasps seemed more dire. Later, we realized that I had something on the inside of me that didn't mesh well with being fourteen thousand feet above sea level. Someone reading this book needs to understand that there is something on the inside of you that is different from those around you. As a result, your elevation will be more strenuous. It will take more out of you. A couple of hours passed, and I realize that I was in trouble. I could not breathe, and organs seem to have the undying pressure. I was suffocating inside. My organs were not getting the adequate oxygen they needed to fully function. I needed oxygen, and I needed it bad! I've learned that we have to be careful of asking to go higher in elevation because the air is thinner and pressure is higher. After a week's stay in the hospital, I was told that I could have fared better if I would have gradually increased in elevation instead of leaving the backroads of Mississippi to go over fourteen thousand feet in elevation. Many people are not ready for the next level of pressure that comes with the next level of leadership. Enjoy the gradual climb and small successes. It's not what you think up here. If you don't slow down, you'll find yourself gasping for air and placing everything you've worked hard for in jeopardy.

WE HAVE TO BE CAREFUL OF ASKING TO GO HIGHER IN ELEVATION BECAUSE THE AIR IS THINNER AND PRESSURE IS HIGHER

The closer proximity one gets to Jesus, the more attacks. There was never a documented incident of the five-thousand or five-hundred being attacked. There is not a mention of Jesus even preparing them for it. When Jesus addressed the seventy, He instructed them that you will be reviled, rejected, and attached. Their assignment was different from the larger group. Some Pastors reading this book should realize that the very nature of your attacks is an indication that you've been promoted. Sometimes your devils tell you when you've been promoted. As you climb the ladder closer to Him, people will attack you to draw likes to their pages. Television shows and blogs will use you as clickbait because your name is valuable. We live in a world that will handle your down moments as an uptick. Christians can be even more vicious. The Army of the Lord is the only army that shoots its wounded instead of ushering them to care and recovery. They place a bullet in their heads and leave them to die alone. The way we care for fallen soldiers must change! Yes, there are some soldiers whose wounds are self-inflicted. They get uplifted in pride and they must get discharged from service. But the wounded soldiers I'm referring to are those who are on the tail end of the rancorous attacks and public persecution. We must do better as a people. We must do better as Christians to love our brothers and sister back to the center. Paul wrote in Galatians Chapter six that:

> Live creatively, friends. If someone falls into sin, forgiv-
> ingly restore him, saving your critical comments for
> yourself. *You* might be needing forgiveness before
> the day's out. Stoop down and reach out to those who
> are oppressed. Share their burdens, and so complete
> Christ's law. If you think you are too good for that, you
> are badly deceived.

Christians should be in the restoration business, not the demolition business. Follow the tenets that Paul spoke about and help restore the next person. You'll never know when you need some grace yourself!

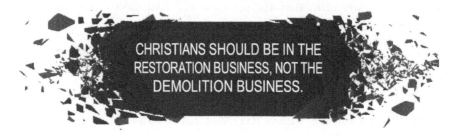

CHRISTIANS SHOULD BE IN THE RESTORATION BUSINESS, NOT THE DEMOLITION BUSINESS.

DISHONORABLE DISCHARGE

---

*You may encounter many defeats, but you must not
be defeated. In fact, it may be necessary to encounter
the defeats, so you can know who you are, what you
can rise from, how you can still come out of it.*

— Maya Angelou

Growing up as a military brat, I was exposed to a lot about military life.
We moved around from state to state and from country to country. I
had an opportunity to see and experience more than the average child.
The military has a distinct culture entirely antithetical to civilian life.
They have their judicial processes and their own systems. When you
serve in the military, you serve at the mercy of the government. In the
pastorate, we serve at the mercy of God; but we also serve at the mercy
of state and federal laws. Additionally, we also serve at the mercy of the
people. Conducive to how one's church is structured, the people may

not vote for things in their church, but they vote with the feet and their money. In the military, one can serve out their contractual commitment, they can retire, or they can be discharged dishonorably. To be released dishonorably means that the army will dismiss a person from service due to criminal or morally unaccepted behavior. Like the military, some Pastors are discharged because of criminal and ethically unaccepted behavior. No one else is to blame. In this chapter, we will explore experiences that lead to a dishonorable discharge. The section will highlight how not all pain is caused by sheep bite. Some discharges are caused because Pastors get from under the guises and the auspices of God's law of morality and the government's laws of acceptable behavior.

POISONED FROM THE ROOTS

One day in 2018, I went to my hometown to take my uncle to a doctor's visit. In his old age, I try to be more active in his life. As we loaded the truck and hit the first corner, he said, "Look at that tree." The tree was the most massive oak tree I had ever seen in my life! It had to be over one-hundred years old. The tree lay comfortably across an old home. A man, who appeared to be the owner, was inspecting the damage. My uncle, after calling the guy's name, said, "Pull over, Chuck." Chuck is one of many childhood nicknames. Don't laugh. I'm sure you have one as well.

Enamored by the size of the tree, I took multiple pictures. I told my uncle that the storm last night must have been powerful enough to uproot such a large tree, causing it to demolish the home that lay crumbling beneath it. My uncle gently grimaced and said, "Nah, I spoke with the guy yesterday. He poisoned the roots of the tree. See, look at how dark the roots are." The man had injected the roots of the large oak with a substance to kill what was holding the tree's strength.

He wanted to get the insurance money from the old house. As I drove away, I thought about Pastors. Sometimes, what we believe caused failure from a distance is a result of something a lot stronger and undetected that impacted matters from the core. Over the years I've served in Christendom, I've had a front-row seat to failure. People saw the wind. I saw the poison.

RIGHT IDEA, WRONG IDEA

All pain is not from the outside. Some discomfort is self-inflicted. Some pain is a result of immaturity or unequipped ministers. One of the greatest travesties is seeing someone attempt to do something that they are not equipped to do. Over the years, I've seen Pastors destroy everything from their families to their finances. Pastoring is one of those professions that will consume you if you allow it to. Having the precious privilege of pastoring other Pastors, I've seen a lot of these mistakes and made my fair share!

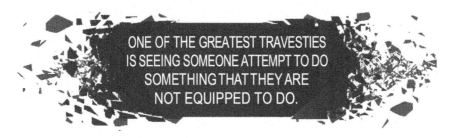

ONE OF THE GREATEST TRAVESTIES IS SEEING SOMEONE ATTEMPT TO DO SOMETHING THAT THEY ARE NOT EQUIPPED TO DO.

SELF-SUFFICIENCY

Ministry, like a business, should be self-sufficient. Understandably, when a person first starts, they will need to incur expenses in their ministry. The church may not have it; therefore, a Pastor may need to have the liquid cash or access to it to cover any unsuspected expenses.

These expenses could be an unsuspecting repair. The costs could span payroll or insurance. Businesses understand this concept. According to the rule of thumb, the business expects to bleed capital for the first three years. Ministries started from the onset can experience this same phenomenon. Even the Internal Revenue Service allows a company to claim three years of a loss.

I've heard unlearned people spout that the ministry is not business. I beg to differ. There are a lot of similarities in practice and principle. Pastors have to be able to read profit-and-loss statements, expense reports, and payroll analysis. Churches have to be equipped with worker's compensation and expected to follow applicable laws of the state and federal governments depending on the structure of the church. Churches have to file certain forms annually, and should have general accounting principles in place. When someone receives cash from the church, that person has to complete an application, W9s, and will receive a 1099 at the end of each year. The church is more like a business than it's not. The IRS expects that there should be a time with an institution that it claims a profit. If it doesn't, that business should close. The same should apply to churches. That notion is not always the case. I've seen Pastors support their budget for up to seven years. They've literally paid to be Pastor. A Pastor having to continually write checks out of their personal banking is not the will of God. It causes strains on their marriages and destroys their finances. I've witnessed Pastors guarantee loans that their church could no longer pay. Now, those Pastors have bankruptcies on their credit rating because they were trying to force a square block into a triangular space.

LEADERSHIP

Pastoring requires a higher level of leadership. Even biblical symbolism calls for Pastors to be shepherds. Shepherds lead. Many Pastors who commence pastoring do not have the leadership qualifications. As a result, they end up mismanaging people, resources, and their personal lives. We see churches close although they had the "it" factor. They may have simply lacked the proper leadership training.

LEADERSHIP IS INFLUENCE.

Additionally, a preaching and teaching gift doesn't signify success as a Pastor. I've witnessed Pastors who could preach someone into a fit but couldn't influence their children. Leadership is influence. It's one's ability to leverage intangible qualities within that enable you to move others to tangible deeds. Over the years, I've had to bear the news to Pastors that it would probably be best if they closed their churches. They tried church growth strategies. They went to church GROW conferences. They read all of the books, but nevertheless they still failed. They were void of the leadership it takes to effectively pastor.

WRONG AREA

The book of Ephesians details what we call the five-fold ministry: Apostles, Evangelists, Teachers, Pastors, and Prophets. Each office has distant characteristics. I've been in ministry for over twenty years. I've seen this cause of failure more than any other purpose. Many people attempt to pastor when they are called to another area of ministry. Many times, when prophets and evangelists get tired of traveling from coast to coast, they open a church to settle down. They are not as effective as they could be because they are not equipped to pastor. One guy I mentored once upon a time fits this case. He is an evangelist. He can preach at revivals and be extremely useful. He flows in the gifts. He is a

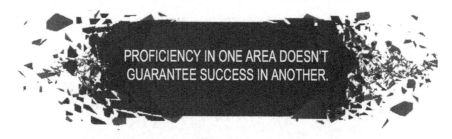

PROFICIENCY IN ONE AREA DOESN'T GUARANTEE SUCCESS IN ANOTHER.

prolific speaker. However, proficiency in one area doesn't guarantee success in another. We see professional athletes attempt to translate achievement in one area to the next. The Pastor could come into a church and uplift the spirits of everyone who hears him speak. He attempted to open a church and couldn't draw twenty people after more than six years of opening. He failed, not because he wasn't equipped to preach, but because he wasn't fit to be a Pastor. Pastoring is more than the articulation of archaic text and the ability to bridge the gap between the original audience and the current one. We face difficulty as leaders getting people planted in their area of purpose. You will not bloom in all soil. You will bloom where He plants you. Sometimes, other people's assignments seem more attractive, but the fact remains, "God will only sustain what He birthed." He is not responsible for maintaining projects that he didn't initiate. Many Pastors are pained because they have attempted to give birth to ventures that God didn't father.

YOU WILL NOT BLOOM IN ALL SOIL. YOU WILL BLOOM WHERE HE PLANTS YOU.

WHEN THE CHURCH HURTS

Over the years, we've seen this notion of "church hurt" mentioned in counseling and social media alike. I'm not debating whether it exists, but I'm introducing a new term in the form of pastoral hurt. Some things can transpire in the lives of Pastors during and before their pastorate that can impact them immensely. I contemplated whether to include this portion in the book. However, many people may have witnessed the wind, but I've seen the roots slowly poisoned over years of service. Had I not taken the step to detox and deconstruct the doctrine I received earlier in ministry, I would not be successful in ministry today.

I've had the opportunity to serve at successful ministries over the past twenty-two years. I've been faithful to that which pertains to another. One church I served as an assistant Pastor, youth Pastor, director of mentoring, and the dean of the Bible college. Yes, I wore many hats. For years, I was Shem and Japheth, covering the nakedness of my leadership. One of the benefits of being around leadership is seeing their carnal moments. For every Pastor reading this book, be careful of who you allow in your space. You need Shems and Japheths to help cover you during your naked moments. For every layperson reading this book, when you become close to your leadership, you'll see Clark Kent a lot more than Superman. You must be mature enough to distinguish the minister in them from the man or woman they are.

I remember our first days at this church. I was oblivious to the notion of what we call today "mega-churches." I was reared in a small Baptist church and moved to medium-size Pentecostal churches. Walking in this church was like going from Walgreens to Super Wal-Mart. They had the lights, the cameras, the fancy seating, stages, and other accoutrements it takes to conduct large productions. I wasn't impressed, but my wife was captivated. On top of the output, the first Sunday we attended, they hosted renowned gospel artists. My wife was sold! We had never been exposed to the likes of such excellence and largeness. We visited several churches in the area, but we eventually came back to that one. We joined and all else was history.

I've worked with youth before coming to this church, so it wasn't long before we found our way to the youth department. The first night we visited youth service, we were spotted by this animated character while walking to take his position to teach. He immediately pulled us to the side after service to converse. It wasn't long before we were teaching the youth, although we had not finished our layperson classes. Leaders who had been there noticed how quickly we were put to service. We weren't seeking positions or notoriety, but when God is in your life, promotion is inevitable.

Months later, my wife and I were summoned to the Bishop's office. I remember the feeling. I remember asking myself the questions: What does he want? What did we do? How does he know us? Walking in that administrative building was like no other. The majestic ambiance of superior construction and the quality of the furniture was intimi- dating on its own. We sat in the administrative assistant's office, which was an office before getting to his office, waiting for him to call us into his personal study. The office was huge. It was something we've only seen on television. We were sitting in the presence of the Bishop! He had researched a lot about us. He had a sheet before him with our credentials, biblical schooling, and other things observed by his senior leadership. He levied question after question. We answered them diplomatically with as few words as possible. I was thinking I'm sitting before "the bishop" who opened multiple churches in cities across the state. At the time, he had the largest African American church in the state and the third-largest church among all ethnicities. He was as big as what the state had to offer. He reared back in his chair and said, "Your future is bright here." He was feeling us because he saw stuff in us that we hadn't seen in ourselves. He finished the meeting by charging us to keep serving and that he would keep watching.

Our ascension was quick. Before I received my ministerial license, I was asked to do a Midweek Service. To understand the gravitas of the assignment, many of the lay ministers either never preached or preached once a year. I was honored to bring the word. I taught a message called "Unstoppable Saints." I heard the CD went platinum in the bookstore. That's an inside joke among the ministers. That night, my gift was validated, and everyone knew I wasn't average. The call I got the next day by the bishop confirmed that he had higher hopes for me. He said I reminded him of another Bishop in the circle who had done well in Florida. He said he wanted to personally train me. We just kept serving. We weren't impressed by ascending to the top because I worked in high capacity in the secular arena. I knew what more senior leadership meant. It meant more responsibility and more problems. It meant attacks from those who coveted the spotlight. I knew that if I was going to deal with the spotlight, I had to deal with the heat

Now, I wasn't on the inside. I was oblivious to the toxicity that existed within the core of leadership. I was a "virgin" to this caliber of ministry. The church was pretty, but basically, it was lipstick on a pig. At that time, I was the director of the Mississippi Department of Health. I was basically doing a full-time job, which was responsible for funding many local health departments across the entire state and doing full-time ministry. I conducted statewide events, preached to youth, recruited and trained leadership, and built youth curriculums, among other things that one of his full-time ministers was paid to accomplish.

As time transpired, I noticed the signs of the death of the ministry before I was brought on full-time. One occasion, I took the youth to a water park in Baton Rouge, Louisiana. They were expecting us. I had gone through the necessary protocols to ensure the proper render payment upon arrival. We had at least fifty kids with us. I went to the front of the line to render payment, and the lady said, "Your card is declined." I told the lady, that must be a mistake. As I ruminate in hindsight, I was thinking, "this is a mega-church, you need to run that card again." Declined! I wasn't in panic mode. I had the money personally to cover the cost, but at this point, I'm thinking, why should I put my money up for bounty when this church has a lot of money? It just so happened that one of the senior leaders was present to use another card that was separate from the main account. I remember that it was American Express. I was calm, the kids didn't know what was going on, and they went on to have a good time. Minutes later, I received a call on my personal cellphone to smooth over what I had witnessed. He laughed and said, "that happens all the time." He indicated how the cards he used when he was a youth Pastor would get declined frequently. He told me not to worry because technical things happen with those cards. I dismissed it and carried on. What I realized is that when you hide something dead, after a while, it begins to stink. My nose was opened, and the smell was in the air.

A couple of months passed, and he called me into the office once again. Now, I had a small guard up because I'd seen stuff. I'd heard things. I tiptoed and completed my assignments; however, the meeting was different. He knew the burden was getting more substantial with me carrying a full-time secular job and doing the work of the ministry. He began the meeting by annihilating one of his leaders who had been with him from day one. He, too, was a native of their hometown. He said, "You're basically doing his job. I want to bring you on full-time. I want you to replace him."

I came from street-level loyalty. There are certain things that you don't say about "day ones." These are people who were with you before the glory days. What he said wasn't false, I just believe he shouldn't have said those things to me. I'm of the firm belief that if a dog brings a bone, he'll carry one, too. He said this guy was the "richest poorest guy he'd known. He will never be successful." Sitting there speechless—not because of the opportunity presented but because he was shedding light on how he really felt about a guy with whom he had much history. I dismissed it. After all, I was speaking with the Bishop! I had an opportunity to do full-time ministry, so we negotiated a salary. I ignored the signs, although I observed them.

DONALD TRUMP

I know! You're curious. While writing this book, the House and the Senate are conducting one of the most extensive impeachment trials in history. Before we knew Donald Trumps as President Trump, the world knew him as a reality television star of "The Apprentice." I remember going to my first staff meeting as an employee. The Bishop was infatuated by Trump. He ran the staff meeting like Donald Trump would run "The Apprentice." I'm not talking about it figuratively; he said he was like Donald Trump, and we were apprentices. I sat there thinking, "What the hell have I gotten myself into!" Yes, I said "hell" and a few other choice words. Don't judge me. I thought to myself that "I left my good government job for this!"

The Bishop would divide the staff into teams, and we were to complete ministerial assignments as if we were on the real "The Apprentice." The team failing would be proverbially fired, and the team completing the task would get affirmation and sometimes gifts. I had studied Myles Munroe, John Maxwell, and other leadership gurus. I knew this wasn't good. As I began to explore his leadership style and the staff followership style, I knew the environment was toxic. He ruled by a "divide and conquer" method. The notion of divide and conquer is to keep the staff at odds with another so that the leader can maintain control. That leadership style results in team members jockeying for position and sabotaging one another at every turn. The staff hated each other. Many of them came to me, but they came to me only once. They learned quickly that coming from a corporate environment, I learned to dot my i's and cross my t's. I could be vicious, but I thought I had escaped that environment. Unbeknownst to me, I had left an environment with sharks to get in the water with piranhas.

It wasn't long before things begin to fall apart. I went on more trips, and more cards were declined. I would make check requests, and the checks written to vendors would bounce. Vendors that had us on thirty-day or fifteen-day net now required payment up front. On payday, it was like the cannonball run to the bank. The last person to the bank found payroll checks would bounce like space jumps. There was a blatant money issue at church, even though offerings would surpass hundreds of thousands a week. Once, on a trip to Rodeo Drive, the Bishop and his cohorts spent thousands in church money. They splurged on items like five-hundred-dollar belts and overpriced shirts. They came back to the office and bragged. One of the guys came and spilled the beans on all the items they bought, plus the credit card bills came in and we saw it. One day I went to the Bishop's house two weeks after Christmas and they had two fifteen-foot trees. They had so many gifts that many were still unopened two weeks after Christmas. These are just some of the things I saw. I won't go into it any further, but I'm attempting to paint a picture of the gross negligence I've witnessed with my own eyes.

REBEL

It was a staff meeting, and I had seen enough. I wasn't vocal anymore, just doing my part to advance to the kingdom. The Bishop had made a statement about Jesus' wealth. He went around the table, asking the staff what we thought. What did he ask me that for? I have a commitment to tell the truth. Respectfully, I said, "Bishop, what you said was biblically inaccurate, and let me tell you why." You could hear a rat breathe in that meeting. There was a haunting silence in the room for at least three minutes. He quickly changed the subject and moved on to the next item. That was the day that changed everything.

I was marked as a "free for all" and "rebel." He knew I had the goods, but he couldn't control me. I realized after surveying the staff, I was the only staff member with advanced degrees. I was the staff member who was accomplished in the secular arena. He needed me. He wanted to plant a church in St. Louis, and he sequestered me to do it. He hated the fact that I didn't bite the company line, but he couldn't deny the anointing on my life. It was about two weeks before everything went down. He called me into his office to tell me of the next steps and how I would benefit. He indicated he was getting ready to fire the Pastor who was in charge of pastoral care. The Bishop besmirched the Pastor's character that day, saying how lazy he was and that he should have never hired him. He talked about how the Pastor had no substance on the inside, but he was well-kept on the outside. I was in total disbelief. At this point, I knew not to nod because it could be misconstrued as an act of agreement. I also thought if he talked about others to me, then surely, I was the topic of conversation when I wasn't in the room. I was young and gullible, but I wasn't a fool. We had seen letters from the bank that had come in calling the church loans because the mortgage was more than three months past due, massive credit card bills, and other signs of financial malfeasance. We had seen him go on open rants about members. I've always been taught that if you don't' say anything, you're complicit. I was vocal when asked. I didn't tell him what he wanted to hear. I told him what I thought from my perspective. If that warranted me being called a rebel, then today, I'm still a rebel. I'll wear that title proudly.

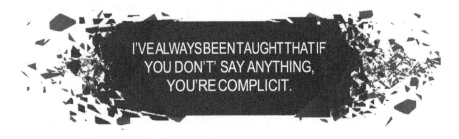

I'VE ALWAYS BEEN TAUGHT THAT IF YOU DON'T' SAY ANYTHING, YOU'RE COMPLICIT.

SOUNDING THE ALARM

I knew this thing was about to come crashing down, but I couldn't go to him as a subordinate. I needed to sound the alarm about what was going on because everyone was in jeopardy. Now, the church didn't have enough money to pay the bills or meet payroll. I called upon one of the long-standing members who was rough around the edges. He was a contractor who later became one of my fishing buddies. In fact, he was also the contractor who built the church. Everyone needs that one person on the team that if cussing is necessary, they will be the one to do it. I told him what was going on and that someone needed to converse with leadership before they lost it all. He took my words at face value and called a meeting the very next day. They met in the Pastor's study next door. I waited close by to find out how they received it. The Bishop and his wife came out of that meeting crying. They knew they had to call their Bishop in Southfield to let them know they had messed this thing up. Within days the Bishop flew down on one of his private jets and took over the entire ministry. By this time, the Bishop had a sexual harassment charge that went public from one of the employees, and the church loan was in default. Did I feel bad about sounding the alarm? No. Something had to be done, or they would have lost it all. The story hit the news, and now the congregants knew that the church and their leadership were in trouble.

RESTORATION

The next week, I and senior leaders met with the Bishop in the Pastor's study. The Bishop was in the next room while he met with the interim Pastor and us. The plan was to have the interim Pastor taking over preaching duties for six months while he restored the Bishop morally. His approach was a biblical concept that is still widely used today. I still have the recordings for these meetings. In fact, I still have documents of everything that I mention in this section, from letters from the bank calling the loan to documentation showing the old building was never paid off entirely. The old loan was capitalized into the new loan even though we had a "burn the note" ceremony.

Nevertheless, we were to resume our duties as usual and send in a list of our responsibilities to the headquarters office in Southfield. Days later, I got a call from the honorable Bishop with a question about my duties. He said, "In thirty years of ministry, I've never seen anyone juggle these many responsibilities effectively." He asked how I could do it. I told him I'm a systems guy. He knew how valuable I was, but he also knew how much influence I had in the church if I was managing all of those ministerial departments. My influence could pose a potential problem. He sent staff down to interview everyone on the team. They need to find out who would be loyal to the interim during the restoration processing.

Weeks went by, and the interim Pastor assumed preaching responsibilities. He was a city-slicker guy with funny-looking suits. The temporary Pastor was smooth, though his city style was often the talk of the congregation. We struck it off. We would talk for hours sometimes about ministry and about the circle we both worked. He didn't know initially how long he would be in Jackson, Mississippi. It was during these conversations that he revealed to me that he was sick. I didn't know how sick until later, but the average person couldn't determine just by his outer appearance. I could imagine the stress of running a mega-church perpetuated the sickness that already plagued his body. In less than two years, my dear friend passed away. In the meantime, the head Bishop from the headquarters office was trying to determine what to do next with the staff. During his deliberations, a letter made its way to the local media stating that a cover-up was happening by the overseeing Bishop. We knew the head of maintenance wrote it. It was written just like he talked, full of grammatical errors and broken linguistics. Immediately, the Bishop at the headquarters changed directions. He issued a statement indicating that he was permanently removing our Bishop from his post.

CLEAN HOUSE

Although the staff knew who wrote it, the Bishop didn't. New leadership knew that cleaning the house with everyone hired from Mississippi would be necessary. The interim Pastor and I were close at the time, so he let me know what was going on ahead of time. I had cleaned out the office. The day came when the bishop in Michigan sent down and security to escort us out of the church as if it was a corporate entity. I wasn't offended, but I cannot deny that I was affected. In fact, the reason I included this section in the book was to accentuate experiences that happened before our pastorate can impact us Pastors. I had never been released from any job, but understand the biblical and political nature of the event. In biblical times, when a new king came into power, they would kill the family and staff of the old regime to prevent an uprising. He was doing just that to prevent a revolt among the existing team, to create a smooth transition for the new Pastor. The interim Pastor was now installed as the permanent Pastor of the church. He later passed away from cancer, which many believed was due to the increased pressure of handling so many issues that came with the transition. He dedicated his life to serving this fellowship. His wife was left to fend for herself. She eventually moved in with her sister. Today, the church has a new Pastor, and the numbers have dwindled to mere hundreds.

LINGERING PAIN

There are still so many issues that stemmed from the removal of the Pastor of the church. Thousands of people were hurt by the fact that they knew something was going on. Many men I know personally vowed to never step foot in another church again. Many of the leaders who were on staff never recovered. The church settled the sexual harassment lawsuit out of court. As for me, I went on to start my current church. Before starting, I had to deal with the pain of being an assistant before effectively pastoring my present church. I went through three-month doctrinal detoxification. I met with Bishops I knew so that they could minister to my soul. I was impacted deeply. One of my mentors indicated that the culture of that church had become more significant than the Christ in me. I promised myself that I would not start the church bleeding. I reviewed my leadership, my doctrine, and even my church growth methodologies. I didn't want to repeat what I had witnessed. Many of the Catholic priests who abused altar boys were abused as altar boys. Victims have a proclivity to victimize. By the time I started the Word Center, I had a renewed sense of self and had wholly removed my past hurt. I successfully transitioned, but many Pastors, even some reading this book, have not. As a result, their churches look and operate like the churches they once served. As a Pastor who may be reading this book, it is essential that you receive wise counsel from someone who can give you a panoramic view of yourself. History doesn't repeat itself; people repeat history. Broken people break other people. As a result, Pastors who have not faced their past, are struggling, and they think they don't have proper church methodologies, the right leaders in place, or the appropriate budget to conduct active ministry. Although in some cases that could be factored in, the issue is that they have lingering pain while attempting to pastor others who are also in pain. *I believe that if you don't heal from what hurt you, you'll bleed on people who didn't cut you.* Consequently, this may be the reason why so many of my people are being destroyed by the church at large. Their Pastor is hurt, and hurting people hurt people.

FALLING ON THE SWORD

As detailed in this chapter, Pastors need healing. Another underlying theme of this chapter is that not all pain is caused by people. Some discomfort is caused because success breeds greed and pride. Pride goes before a fall. If I spoke in detail about all that happened, no person reading this book would be the same. The Western Church is in crisis. It's not always at the fault of wayward and sick membership. Sometimes it's because of untrained, unprepared, and unhealed leadership. Sometimes, the pain that the Pastor experiences is self-inflicted. They can blame the parishioners, the community, the haters, and other outside influences, but as Pastors, we must look introspectively and take responsibility for our actions. To this day, that Pastor who fell from grace still blames everyone, including myself for his failure. I wasn't in charge of the finances. I wasn't over his executive leadership team. I didn't influence him to harass anyone. I was a leader who didn't go with the flow. Later, his Bishop from Michigan stood before his congregation and told them that everyone he released was unqualified to be in their position. By default, his conjecture included me, although I was the Director of the four-year Bible college, youth Pastor, assistant Pastor, director of the ministry of helps, and director of mentoring, among other duties. Although he made the statement publicly, by his volition he indicated I was freak of nature in the ministry. I could have taken it personally, but he needed to take responsibility that he didn't require continuing education for one of his Pastors whose church outgrew his character. A Pastor may be reading this book now and blaming everyone else for these missteps, miscalculations, and mismanagement. Could it be that you are not a casualty of pain inflicted by sheep? Could it be that you fell on your own sword? It's time for you to eat from the sermons you preach others.

THE UNGRATEFUL NINE

---

*If a fellow isn't thankful for what he's got, he isn't
likely to be thankful for what he's going to get.*

— Frank A. Clark

One of the most eye-opening stories in the Bible is the story of the ten
lepers. Many Pastors who are reading this book will attest to this chapter. Many parishioners know already it as they matriculated through
Sunday School. With many congregants, or those outside of the church,
jaws may drop at the Pastoral abuse that occurs on a regular basis.
Maybe you're not familiar with the story. Let me refresh your memory.
The seventeenth chapter of the book of Luke states:

> While He was on the way to Jerusalem, He was passing
> between Samaria and Galilee. As He entered a village,
> ten leprous men who stood at a distance met Him; and

they raised their voices, saying, "Jesus, Master, have mercy on us!" When He saw them, He said to them, "Go and show yourselves to the priests." And as they were going, they were cleansed. Now one of them, when he saw that he had been healed, turned back, glorifying God with a loud voice, and he fell on his face at His feet, giving thanks to Him. And he was a Samaritan. Then Jesus answered and said, "Were there not ten cleansed? But the nine—where are they? Was no one found who returned to give glory to God, except this foreigner?" And He said to him, "Stand up and go; your faith has made you well."

Jesus' encountered ten lepers. To undergird the context of the story above, one must understand the condition of the leper. This dreaded disease degenerated its victims and eventually proved fatal. No cure for it was known. In Israel, lepers were generally isolated from non-lepers, but this was not always the custom in other nations, including Aram. The lepers met Jesus as He was entering the city, after coming in from a long trip. The lepers had no idea where He was going: He could have been heading for an important meeting, or He could have been tired and exhausted, or He could have had no time for interruptions, but the lepers did not care. They were so desperate they would interrupt Him no matter what. When you're desperate, you don't have the time for the details. Although they were desperate, they weren't disrespectful. The lepers "stood at a distance." They understood and respected the law, which demanded they stand at least six feet away from a person. These lepers were many yards away from Jesus because of the large crowd following Him. They showed great respect for the law by remaining on the outskirts of the group. On other occasions, those needing healing had ignored the law, bursting through crowds and running up to Jesus.

Jesus was bound to note their humility and their acknowledgment of being unclean. Their need was not for instruction, so they didn't call him Rabbi. They needed him for healing, and by healing, they meant both the cleansing of their physical bodies and the sin that had caused their infirmity. The Jews always connected leprosy with the sin of the person. They recognized Jesus to be the Master who could cleanse both the spirit and body. Jesus was one who could give them both healing and forgiveness of sins. Although they came asking for one thing, Jesus gave them more!

HELP!

These men were in trouble physiologically, emotionally, socially, and spiritually. Many people who grace the doors of the church are in similar predicaments. Their finances are in trouble, their marriage is on life support, and their lives are in shambles. As Pastors, our job is to help throw the life jacket with the expectancy to keep people from drowning. We are to be extensions to what Jesus indicated He was called to do in the fourth chapter of Luke:

> The Spirit of the Lord is upon Me,
> Because He anointed Me to preach the gospel to the poor.
> He has sent Me to proclaim release to the captives,
> And recovery of sight to the blind,
> To set free those who are oppressed,
> To proclaim the favorable year of the Lord.

We are in the business of restoration. Any faithful Pastor can attest that we help people. The obstacle and the challenges we face are that we help people who won't help themselves. We can succeed in recovery for people who genuinely want help. The lepers cried out of support.

They weren't on Jesus' agenda, but when you have the heart to heal, you extend olive branches to people with whom we don't have personal relationships. Jesus healed all ten lepers. The healing is evident when he indicated that they show themselves to the priest. According to *Luke: An Introduction and Commentary*, the author states, "Apparently, Jesus did not see them at first, but when he did, he responded." He did not come to them or touch them. He did not even say, "You are cured!" He told them, leprous as they were, to go and show themselves to the priests, the standard procedure when a leper was cured. The priest operated as a kind of health inspector to verify that the healing had, in fact, taken place. Jesus was putting their faith to the test by asking the men to act as though they had been cured. And as they obeyed so it happened: as they went, they were cleansed. The highlight of the story is when one returned to say, "Thank you" before the priest validated his healing. As a result, Jesus gave him more than he desired. He gave him wholeness. Even though the Pastor helps to usher in change to many people's lives, we run into barriers. It seemed that helping people would yield favorable results. I've come to learn that in ministry, help has a short memory. Pastors can open their homes, their minds, their hearts, and the wallets, and we still get bit by the bitterness of the people we help.

HELP HAS A SHORT MEMORY.

In this chapter, I want to highlight the ungrateful nine who had their life changed with an encounter with leadership. The nine represent more than just ungratefulness. They represent the people who turn on their administration, after all they have done. The chapter describes the maliciousness of current and former members. Also, every person who leaves a church is not wrong. In fact, we teach members how to depart the ministry during our membership process. We must be thankful for the time that people give us. It happens all too often that situations like this leave the Pastor hurt or bitter. The stories I tell in this chapter are not all things that happened at my ministry, but nevertheless, they are true, yet they represent only a micro-example of what Pastors must endure. Additionally, they are not intended to expose anyone; they are to enlighten the readers of the past abuses that happen at the hands of congregants. The aim is that congregants would be more aware and more sensitive to the things they do and say.

I once led a couple through a divorce. I was more acclimated with the young lady, considering I knew her longer than the husband, yet I offered advisement to them both. This was a painful divorce. Both had thriving businesses. Kids were involved, and both had become bitter over the process of separation. I was there for prayer, advisement, instruction, and consultation among everything else. Pastors have to be comforters. We comfort people in times of extreme stress and their darkest moments. I opened my home, I took time from my family to help make comfort during the process. The divorce took a couple of years, and it was final. The young man moved on. The lady ultimately sold her practice for millions. It seems that as a grateful gesture of saying thanks, she might have said, "Here is something to help with your vision," considering that everyone in the city knew that our church was in dire need of a larger facility. We never received a dime or a "thank you" for our help. She moved her membership to the church down the street, which happens to be pastored by an amazing gentleman, whom I respect dearly. I'm sure his ministry was a benefactor, while we inherited her burdens. This is the plight of many Pastors across the country.

We know all too well the investment we make, while other people or ministries receive the harvest.

I have some relational expertise, and as a result, I draw a lot of single ladies to the ministry. We've had some good people come through our doors. They have extended their time, talents, and treasure to help advance the kingdom. We had this one young lady who was a great poet. We've done so many projects together for the church and the city. We've posted this young lady on our platforms to give her notoriety to the nations. Our modus operandi is to treat people well and extend existential help when needed. It's not abnormal to provide preferential treatment to those who serve, that are present and are active in helping with the vision. When a request for assistance came in for this young lady, I knew the answer would be "yes" by the committee who shares the responsibility of approving emergency assistance. We helped get her out of a tight spot.

A month or so passed, and she seemed to disappear. I contacted her via telephone and Facebook Messenger. We had a normal conversation, and she indicated that she was just busy. Another month passed, and my wife asked had I seen her. My wife contacted her as well. Each month, for four to five months, we checked up on her as we do periodically with people we haven't seen in a while. One day I get a screenshot from someone saying, look what this lady posted. She had posted that she was going to the one specific church. The post indicated that she had been missing for four months, and no one contacted her. I wish I could insert the opened-eyed smiley right here. Shock didn't describe the feeling I had. We had messages and logs of our contacts with her. We had receipts. The post gained a lot of traction, and although she didn't name us, people in the city knew she went to our church. Thankfully, people who knew us knew that was reaching for attention. They knew she was lying. She lost friends and associates from that post because we had "receipts." The bottom line is that she was leaving the church anyways because she was supposedly marrying a minister. She hustled us in the process and started a mess on the way out. We were baffled at how a person could blatantly lie to get attention. We may never know the truth, and the reality is that we are not searching for it.

One story is of a family who left a church they had attended for years. The Pastor knew them, and they knew the Pastor. They left without notifying the Pastor, which I believe is dishonorable. They decided to join a large church in the city that was the hottest place to join. They had been gone over a year. Something happened to their son that resulted in his death. They went to the new Pastor, requesting that he eulogize their son. The Pastor told him that he didn't know them, and so he wasn't going to eulogize their son, but they could use the church for a fee. The grieving family went back to their old church and requested their former Pastor eulogize their son. He hadn't heard from them since the last service he saw them, which was over a year prior. He indicated he was busy and would not be able to eulogize their son. The Pastor stated that they should contact their Pastor personally and request that he do it. He then proceeded to tell them he had to run to a meeting and hung up. Later that day, the grieving family went on social media and blasted their previous Pastor for not eulogizing their son. These types of posts get a lot of traction, and thousands chimed in to affirm their position and even to tell their stories. They never mentioned they asked their current Pastor, and that the Pastor indicated that he didn't know them. Or that their new church was attempting to charge them for the funeral. Pastors are on the tail end of vicious attacks like this one that often play out on social media. Frequently, Pastors won't be able to present adequate defense due to the viral nature of negative posts.

ET TU, BRUTE?

One of the most devastating pains that a Pastor experiences is when someone they trusted and trained become a traitor. A traitor is a person who betrays a friend or principle. Conversing with Pastors across the country, this is something that Pastors never get accustomed to. I've garnered stories from multiple Pastors. In the ten years I've been in the pastorate, I've had my shared of "let downs," disappointments, and betrayals. I have people I've invested into dearly turn their backs as if we've never met and attack like I was a bitter enemy. Betrayal is not just a menial event, but it's devastating. It's distressing because only people you trust can betray you. If a pastor is not careful, betrayal can change their perspective and cause to them to pastor with a cold heart.

ONLY PEOPLE YOU TRUST CAN BETRAY YOU.

PROJECTION

Eight years ago, I met a young lady who was lost and suffering deep pains of her past. She was somewhat of a loner. She had deep-seated emotional issues and could barely contain herself. People saw her problems; I saw a diamond in the rough. I saw what she could potentially become if she would be able to overcome the obstacles she once faced in her life. We drew her in and help restore her to be effective in the kingdom. We treated her like a daughter. When she needed to meet, we met. When she needed to talk, we would open up our ears to hear. Eventually, we cultivated the young lady's gifts. She worked steadily and hard for the kingdom. My wife and I would see traces of her old life spring up like Jason on Friday the thirteenth. We knew that she would be a work in progress like we all are works in progress. We noticed another trend. She was fired from every job that that held. There was always drama involved. Although nothing, at first, transferred to the church, we noticed the pattern over the years. Eventually, what was going on outside the church begin to bleed on the parishioners. What was going on with her father began to get projected on us. When she was fired from another job, I get a text saying, "you were never there for me." I was baffled, as Comedian Ha Ha Davis would say. The same person who we gave opportunity after opportunity. The same one we embraced when others left her to fend for herself. I stepped back from the situation and realized that all the toxic stuff she stated, which is not listed above in its entirety, had nothing to do with us. She was projecting her unresolved hurt with her biological parents on us.

Projection is a psychological term that people use as a defense mechanism to cope with feelings, emotions, and thoughts. They direct these undesirable feelings and emotions onto someone else rather than dealing with the real issue or people who caused the feelings and emotions. It is simplified by having a bad day at work and coming home to kick the cat. The cat wasn't the originator of the feelings and emotions; it was the recipient of unresolved hurt. Pastors and Pastor's wives, in many cases, are the individuals who receive the punishment for unresolved issues. Members like the ones mentioned above, either don't have access to the parents that caused the anguish or they don't dare to face them. Pastors become easy targets due to parental problems. There are times when we do mess up. We may not speak or hug a member due to the many goings and comings of our day. We may forget to call during their special day. Any little mishap can trigger a crisis in those who don't want to deal with the dysfunctions of their past.

Needless to say, eight months later, she sent a message on social media apologizing for everything and realized that we had nothing to do with the negatives in her life. It sounds like projection to me!

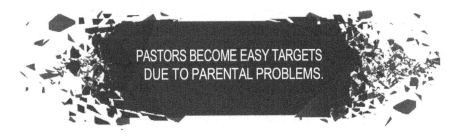

PASTORS BECOME EASY TARGETS DUE TO PARENTAL PROBLEMS.

THE MOM FACTOR

Dr. Henry Cloud and Dr. John Townsend wrote a great book called *The Mom Factor*. The book states that no one has influenced the person you are today like your mother. The way she handled your needs as a child has shaped your world view, your relationships, your marriage, your career, and your self-image—your life. They mentioned various types of mothers, such as the "Phantom Mother." The Phantom Mother is the mother who was there but not there. Many times she was detached both physically and emotionally. Because of her emotional issues, she struggled with communicating and being fully present. As a result, she is likely to pass those emotional issues down to her children. Then there is the "Controlling Mom." The problem with this type of mother is that because she was so strict, the child couldn't wait to get free. As a result, this child was wild in college and made more mistakes because they weren't parented with balance. At some point, you must give your child room to make mistakes while they are in your house so that when they make a mistake outside of your home, it won't be so devastating. The point of the book is that whatever relationship one has or had with their mother helps define all other relationships. If in your eyes, your mother didn't love you, you perceive that nobody does. The great news, the authors indicate, is that one can identify areas that need reshaping, to make positive choices for personal change, and to establish a mature relationship with their Mom today, and ultimately help your relationship with your daughter tomorrow.

Because of the Mom Factor, many Pastor's wives or what we call first ladies are on the receiving end of whatever relationship that person had with their mother. The difference is that there is often less grace for spiritual parents than there are for biological parents. Members often magnify our mistakes while minimizing their biological parents' faults. As harsh as this reality sounds, this is a reality that many of us Pastors face all too often. Once, one of my assistants couldn't meet with a couple he had met with six times prior because he had to work his part-time job to provide extra for his family. She wanted to meet that week, and he couldn't. He couldn't meet that week because of his schedule. He conversed with her two weeks after it, and she indicated she was angry with him and that he was two weeks too late. She left the church because she didn't get her way. Before you get mad at something petty that your Pastor or first lady did or didn't do, ask yourself, "Does this infraction warrant this type of anger?" Your biological parents did more, and you still love them, right? Keep that same energy with us.

CAN'T BE TRUSTED

When a Pastor first starts a church from nothing, they are more likely to make more mistakes because they must filter through much more. We were growing fast. People were coming indicating they wanted to help. We didn't know who to trust, but welcomed the help. Our inaugural year, we had a couple of seniors. This one senior in particular came over who was a handful, but helpful. The woman could cook tree bark and make it taste delicious. She was also one of those cussing saints. You didn't want to cross her. She could cuss so good that it would rhyme coming out. At that time, we were small enough to have food often on special occasions. It was only natural that we garner her assistance. Word would get back to us about nasty and offensive remarks in front of first-time guests and other workers. People became uncomfortable in her presence. We addressed every issue as it came up. One problem, in particular, was the final straw. We noticed how she hinted at specific events and issues that were going on around the church. These items were private. They were only relegated to senior leadership. How did she know? Who told her? Some of this stuff wasn't even church-related? Was she some type of prophetess or something?

At that time, my daughter was a little over two years old. Like many parents, my wife would let her use the phone to hold her attention while completing important tasks. We discovered that this senior would catch my daughter and look through my wife's text messages. She knew things that nobody else knew because she had access to what others didn't have access to. She was accessing our private messages. Some people just can't be trusted! Needless to say, we asked her to leave the church. To date, this was the only member we've asked to leave. Let me stop to pick up your mouth because it's most likely on the floor by now. I'm just touching the surface of some of the pain we endure.

JUST UNGRATEFUL

There are so many stories I can tell you of ungratefulness, but this one in particular stands out. There was a guy I've known for some time. He was a barber, but he didn't have his license. He would bounce from shop to shop, cutting in the back rooms to avoid the board inspections that periodically happen in barbershops. A barbershop caught with barbers not properly licensed could be fined the first infraction and penalized up to one thousand dollars on multiple offenses. The barber can also be taken to jail. This guy had been cutting over fifteen years. He had started barber school but dropped out. He was just as talented as many other barbers who were licensed, but he didn't have their credentials.

After conversing with him, I asked why he didn't just get his license. He indicated how many hours he needed, and he didn't have the finances to go to back to the barber school and make enough to make ends meet. As mentioned earlier, as Pastors, we are called upon to provide insight in areas other than spiritual matters. Our goal is to enrich the lives of those we lead. I made a call to an old friend who owns a barber school. I told him about the situation facing one of my parishioners and his tangible ability to cut. Off the strength of my name, he met with him. He further proceeded by assisting him in getting his license and allowed him to take the final test. My friend even waived the test fees. After fifteen years, this young man received his barber's license because his Pastor vouched for him to a longtime friend. The young barber never said "thank you" to me or the barber school owner who went out on a limb for him. I've only seen him on a few occasions over the years since.

MARTHA ATTITUDE/MARY TESTIMONY

Our church has been used to radically change people's lives. We've ushered people from depression and other emotional lows to pulling people from toxic environments such as domestic violence and sex trafficking. We help people find housing, jobs, even occasionally play cupid. As echoed earlier, help has a short memory. There are those whose lives are walking testimonies like that of Mary of Magdalene. According to historical text, many theologians believe that she may have been the woman caught in adultery. Others think that she was a lady of the evening, and Jesus rescued her from a life of promiscuity. As a result, there was nothing she wouldn't do to help advance the Kingdom of God. She was grateful. Martha, on the other hand, was often so caught up working for the Lord that she didn't minister to the Lord. Our ministry has had our share of Marys and Marthas.

WHEN PASTORS SAY "NO"

A good friend who pastors a progressive church in Florida recently had a run-in with a Martha. They had literally changed this person's life spiritually and existentially. As a result of the young man's connection to the Pastor, he lived an enriched life. My friend had planted churches throughout his city and placed Pastors in them to facilitate the campus. After watching many others get sent to satellite churches, he wanted to get a shot as well. The young man's heart grew cold. He had access to everything. My friend would send him to the conferences he wanted. He would give him a portion of honorariums that he accumulated while traveling. He would even train the young man in secular areas to create different streams of income. On an unsuspecting day, the young man sent out a letter to all the workers in the church, speaking about the Pastor in a negative light. It caused massive confusion in his staff. As Pastors, we can mold people who may not be as anointed or talented, but we have nothing to help turn an evil heart.

THE WORLD WOULD BE A BETTER PLACE IF PEOPLE LIVED WHAT THEY POSTED.

I once had a person who had to correct. He had severe heart issues. I told him that he shouldn't post stuff that's not reflective of who he really is. The world would be a better place if people lived what they posted. The guy pretended to have a certain level of lifestyle while not being able to pay his mortgage. He insulted others, calling them broke while not having adequate resources to take care of his own family. Many congregants are okay with their Pastor until he has to correct them or tell them no. Pastors are supposed to pastor sheep, not wolves. We can always tell the nature of the animal when we fix it. A sheep will never growl back you, but when you poke at the wolf, he'll show his teeth.

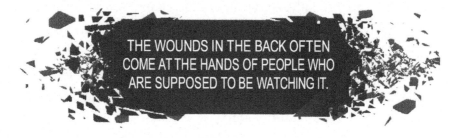

THE WOUNDS IN THE BACK OFTEN COME AT THE HANDS OF PEOPLE WHO ARE SUPPOSED TO BE WATCHING IT.

The stories above are simply some of the stories so that readers can get an understanding of the heartache and pain that Pastors must endure. The pain often comes from people we've helped the most. The wounds in the back often come at the hands of people who are supposed to be watching it. The stories are so expansive and so many in number, an entire book could be written on the betrayal, disloyalty, and ungratefulness Pastors experience during their pastorate. Despite the constant pain this causes, there is nothing like the one coming back to say, "Thank you." There is nothing like being appreciated for the things that you do. Although appreciation is not required, sometimes Pastors need to know that they are impacting some one's life.

Years ago, I got permission to tell this young lady's story. It's a story of impact and gratefulness. When we initiated the church, our ministry was small enough to notice just about everything. Let start by telling you that we built our department by reaching the unsaved, the forgotten, and those a little rough around the edges. During service, I noticed how some of the men had huddled in the back, whispering among themselves. They indicated that the young lady who was in the audience was a known dancer at a local strip club. Before you judge with disdain, everyone is an "ex" something.

I wanted to ask how they knew, but I didn't bother. I already knew. The lady kept coming and eventually joined. I remember early in our ministry, making the statement that no matter where you are in life, you can advance. I said, "You're two years away from an associate's degree, four years from a bachelor's degree, six years from a master's degree, and eight or nine years from a Ph.D. Just start!"

The young lady heard those sentiments and took those words and ran. She went to school and in a couple of years, received her master's degree in counseling. As a single mother, things could be a little hard. She was able to get a job out of state that would help support her family in its entirety. The church had changed her life. Already a vocal person, she let the people know that my church had changed her life. She was the one who came back and said, "Thank you." I'll never forget her and to this day. Like a proud father yielding and watching the accomplishments of a daughter who no longer lives in the house. That one "Thank you" is worth enduring the nine who didn't say anything.

THE FIRST FAMILY

"Other things may change us, but we start and end with the family."

— *Anthony Brandt*

The majority of the Pastors in American are married. In talking about the Pastors, we often forget to mention those who support the Pastor behind the scenes. A Pastor's church is only as healthy as the support they have around them, especially their immediate family. People have written books on preachers' kids (PKs) and the many struggles they endure growing up in ministry. I've seen very few works that deal with the plight and pain of the first lady and the first family. I've decided to add a short chapter that deals with some of the pain and realities of being a Pastor's wife.

UNREALISTIC EXPECTATIONS

Everyone has their ideology on who and what a first lady should be. Their idea is based on the Pastor's wife in the church they attended as a child. In most cases, this first lady was not vocal. She was not expected to carry out sacerdotal functions, events, or chats with ladies. She sat on the front row like a pretty little flower. People knew she was there, but she wasn't a force in the church. Unlearned Pastors would send their wives to correct members when necessary and put out fires as if she was the church fire marshal. As a result, people in the old church loved their Pastor but hated the first lady. The Pastor often used her as a sheepdog, so there was always dissension between the lady of the house and the congregants. Fast-forward thirty years later: Things have changed immensely.

The first lady is not the pretty little flower in a beautiful dress and big hat that sits on the front row anymore. A lady's role, due to the women's liberation movements, has evolved immensely. Pastor's wives are now expected to carry their share of the weight, yet often don't get their share of the praise when things go right. The expectations for twenty-first century Pastor's wives are heightened. People no longer just call meetings with the Pastor. They want to meet with the first lady. They want her counsel and wisdom. They require her time and knowledge. Frequently, the first lady is not full-time. Therefore, she has to balance the duties of the home with that of the church. We'll discuss that further in another section.

People expect the first lady to be a modest dresser but not look too old. Her attire comes under the scrutiny of critical eyes. Baring too much skin, she looks like someone off the street. If she is covered, people will say she seems old like the Our wives are not the Pastor's wives in the churches we attended as children. People watch the brands she wears, the purses she totes, and the shoes on her feet. As with the Pastor, if the first lady wears a brand they can't afford, she is doing too much. Like that of the Pastor, the member's wardrobe is often the barometer for the first lady's closet. The first family is always under the duress to find the happy medium of not angering someone.

In addition to these elements, a Pastor's wife in the twenty-first century is also expected to host events. Ladies want girl talk, girl chat, lady's night out, and other things to engage in areas of a woman's life. Some even want women's conferences. These types of occurrences are great, but those who simply attend do not know the amount of time and energy that goes into such events. My wife, in the past, hosted a fashion show called Fashion Unleased. She held this event annually. It grew to nearly five hundred in attendance. I've witnessed what it took to make such an event successful with excellence. They had vendors that sold products. She had to get people to host or even an occasional entertainment act. She had to encourage boutiques to donate clothing. She had to deal with contracts with facilities. We had to hire people for sound and lighting. On top of the logistics, we had to have models that would fit the clothing provided by the boutiques. The process took a considerable amount of staff. We had to have greeters, backstage transition teams, seaters, security, parking attendance, and other volunteers to host this live event. Depending on the size of the church, the first lady is involved in many endeavors to make any occasion successful. Keep in mind, the first lady often doesn't work for the church. She does tasks like these despite potentially having a job and balancing family and regular ministerial duties.

FIRST MINISTRY

Often people forget that the Pastor's wives have a family. Like children, members warrant attention. The wife may have two or three children, but the entire women's congregation becomes her extended children. Like that of her biological children, if they don't get the required attention, they throw tantrums. We've had people get angry at my wife because she couldn't meet with them in the week they requested. They quickly forget that her family is her first ministry. On top of that, my wife is a Nurse Practitioner over an entire department. Imagine that! Working full time, maintaining family, supporting in ministry, and getting pulled upon by the people. Where is her personal time?

SHARED SPOUSE

When a woman is married to a Pastor, it requires her to be extremely unselfish. The Pastor is never truly off. We're on call twenty-four hours a day. One who is called to the pastorate doesn't have a nine-to-five job. Understand that we get calls during the middle of the night by people in crisis or to notify us that someone has transitioned to death. Many of us still conduct hospital visits. We do weddings and funerals regularly. We have meetings with community leaders and other dignitaries when called upon. A Pastor's job is never indeed done. New people die, and others get married. Churches of my size have managed to hire staff to help alleviate these types of responsibilities, but some functions require a senior leader to be present. If a Pastor and his wife have kids, they must attend their events. One of the worst things a Pastor can do is not be present for a child at the expense of the church. The child can ultimately grow up and become bitter toward the institution that took their father. They are not able to separate whether something is essential. They are only able to determine that their father is not there and missed an important milestone in their lives. As Pastors, we must show our families that they are first place. We can't lose our families at the expense of building the church. Scripture makes this principle clear. What good is it for a person to gain the world and lose their soul? In other words, what good is it for a person to build the church and lose their family? That's not God's heart. In the Old Testament, newly married soldiers were required to take a year off to minister to the need of their families. That's God's heart. Don't lose your family fighting in the army of the Lord. Find time to minister to them and give them your undivided attention.

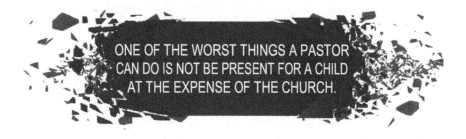

ONE OF THE WORST THINGS A PASTOR CAN DO IS NOT BE PRESENT FOR A CHILD AT THE EXPENSE OF THE CHURCH.

ROASTED PASTOR

Earlier in the book, I mentioned many of the hardships that the Pastor endures. Who do you think has to be there when members are serving roasted Pastor with a side of disloyalty? Who has to be there when people they've trained and invested in turn their back to do the unthinkable? Who do you think is there to hear the cries when the Pastor is pregnant with vision, but is aborted by lack? Who do you think has to bear a listening ear when things aren't going well? Yes, his wife. As a married couple, you're one flesh. When they roast the Pastor, they cook the first lady. She must hear people's complaints and see the pain they inflict and come to church and smile.

Being a Pastor's wife is just as much of calling as being the Pastor. They walk together. They excel together. They even lose together. It's impossible to win together and lose separately. When a Pastor takes arrows in the back, she is the one who pulls them out and medicates the pain. They see and hear just as much as the Pastor. As a congregant reading this book, celebrate her and the children. Don't forget to add them to the program during anniversaries. When the Pastor pains, they all sting. They deserve all that the senior Pastor receives and more!

IT'S IMPOSSIBLE TO WIN TOGETHER
AND LOSE SEPARATELY.

MUSICIAN MADNESS

*"Music gives a soul to the universe, wings to the mind,
flight to the imagination and life to everything."*

— Plato

There has been a long-standing love/hate relationship between Pastors and musicians. There is the age-old debate relating to payment of musicians and whether they should be members of the church in which they play. I've heard Pastors talk about their work ethic, punctuality, spiritualty, among other things that clergy consider essential. Some also entertain the notion that musicians shouldn't be committed to more than one church. Regardless of the age-old and emerging issues, dealing with musicians can cause just as much pain as dealing with congregants. I'm sure musicians would say the same as it relates to Pastors. In fact, I'll personally ask musicians to chime in on my social media pages to give a balanced view of their issues with churches. I've witnessed and heard of nightmare experiences with Pastors dealing with them. In this chapter, I aim to give light to some of the challenges we face in working with them but provide relief on how to handle situations before they occur.

THE BIBLE BELT

At the genesis of my church, I expected to deal with the usual frivolities of new church plants. Financial worry, attendance pendulums, low cash flow, and staffing issues are among significant issues that new Pastors face. Unlike some new ministries, I decided to start with a full band and singers. Looking back in hindsight, I had no clue about what I was about to embark upon.

Mississippi rests in what's called the "Bible Belt." The church experience is unique in Southern states. Music is not just important, but a pivotal factor in the services of a church. Churches without active music departments, but great preaching, are often overlooked by people looking to plant their families in churches. The music factor may not be as crucial in other areas of the country, but one cannot overlook this notion in the Bible Belt.

Before starting our church, I knew that music was a big deal. I had to seek out those who were already in the industry. I needed a band and singers. Not knowing exactly what was the going rate for musicians, I had to take a dive into the endeavor with little to no experience. For the first couple of months, I paid singers, a keyboard player, and a drummer. I hired them with no preconceived idea of what my yearly budget would be, but I knew I wouldn't survive without them because in the Bible Belt, music is a principle thing.

BUDGET BUSTERS

In the first couple of months of our ministry, I got a realistic idea of what it takes to have a full band. Money began to disappear like items in a Chris Angel magic show with the exception that there was no magic wand or abracadabra. It was merely musicians with their hands held out. I paid the singers, the band, the security, the school to rent, insurance, and accounting, just to name a few of the items in the budget. To place things in perspective, I wasn't planted by an organization. I wasn't installed by a renowned Bishop. The budget consisted of what was in my wife and my savings account. We purchased everything! A church, just like a new business, many times will have to bleed capital until there are enough donations to support the operation. Salaries for the Pastor and staff are an afterthought unless a Pastor explodes exponentially like some churches around the country. These churches are not the norm; they are the aberration. Our money started to look funny and the change was looking strange. I did what any businessman would do. I cut them. I cut them all and went on the hunt for some more reasonable musicians who could work with a new church.

CULTURAL SNAFU

As a new church, it was way more difficult to find new musicians. Musicians, because of pastoral abuses, were skeptical about working with new churches. I was told by musicians that when my church grows, they would consider it. Interestingly enough, by year three, people were knocking on my door to play.

As our church began to grow, so did the opportunity to hire better musicians. We had a little more money to invest in equipment and training. I paid musicians according to the going rate in our geographical location. I remember one instance when the church met at an old theme park called "The Park on Lakeland." The place used to be filled with kids and adults waiting in line to play miniature golf, ride go-carts, and play video games and laser tag. I thought it was the perfect situation, but the location wasn't conducive to my target population. I remember hiring this keyboard player. He seemed like he would be a great fit. He was probably my fourth keyboard player. I made sure that he was compensated fairly for his time even though in good conscience, looking back in hindsight, I couldn't afford to pay him that salary.

After a couple of months, he begins to levy complaints about pay. I noticed he was later for church than usual, barely showing for up for practice, giving minimal effort, and so on. I did what any person running any organization would do: I fired him. He left my church and went to a larger-sized church pastored by a great brother. You're thinking, what is wrong with that? The church I'm referencing doesn't pay their musicians. He left my church, which was a start-up, because he wasn't paid more, only to donate his time at a larger church. To date, he still plays for this church for free.

There is a cultural conundrum that reeks in churches in America. Sunday is said to be one of the most segregated times of the week. The segregation flourishes in the music as well. It is well known that churches pastored by Caucasians request that musicians donate their time to the kingdom. The churches most likely have musicians who double as engineers, doctors, lawyers, and so on, giving their gift to the church. This is not to suggest that those professionals don't give their time in other culture settings. It's more prevalent in evangelical and progressive Caucasian churches. As a result, these churches are allowed to grow financially because they can allocate a larger portion of their budget in other areas include marketing and new member assimilation. The contrapositive is that churches led by African American Pastors have to designate a significant part to musicians. As a result of the musician element, African American churches often grow at slower rates and paces. We allocate at least one-third of our budget to music.

The differences in cultures stem from early socialization. African Americans at old ages receive teachings that inculcate them to find a gig and to earn money from their gifts. Although they are biblically accurate, the "gig" is often placed over sowing the gift. The notion of misplacement of kingdom priorities often smothers ministries with costs that could allow the churches to grow and ultimately lead to compensation of the musicians. Other cultures teach giving back. The whole notion of gifting the ministry often will lead older members to even endow the churches with portions if not all of their insurance when they expire from the earth. The truth is that African American led churches do start off further behind than Caucasian led churches. Without putting on my sociological hat, I'll say the disparities are worth mentioning. Although there are other factors, money is one of the most critical factors advancing the mission of any organization. We may never totally understand all of the complexities of cultural differences within the musician world, but they exist, and we can no longer ignore them. It's time for the church at large to have a serious conversation about the divided church that preaches about a unified kingdom

INDISPENSABLE

As mentioned earlier, in the Bible Belt, music is a critical part of any worship service. Without it, many won't give a second thought to visiting or joining. Why are musicians so important? Why should musicians get paid? Should Pastors require them to donate their gift and be a part of the ministry? One can find the answer in the indispensability of the gift offered to the church.

In smaller ministries, it's not uncommon for members to serve in multiple positions. The usher may also work the sound. A greeter may also work in the parking lot. Many of the positions, like those mentioned, are detached from intellectual abilities and giftings. One can teach a person to smile and hug each person coming into the building. One can teach a person the various buttons on the soundboard. One can lay out a plan for the workers to park people adequately and, at the same time, render five-star customer service. However, no one can jump on the percussions or keyboard.

In many cases, it takes years for musicians to develop their gifts and skillsets to effectively coordinate with vocals and other instruments. Some take lessons, while others form expertise through hours or practicing in what's known as shedding. If a keyboard player doesn't show up, then they are not easily replaced by individuals in other areas. The drummer can greet, park, or run the sound. The sound personnel, unless trained, cannot jump on the drums or the bass and play on demand. The concept is rooted in simple supply and demand. If the supply is low and the demand is high, the worth and value of the service or product becomes premium. If anyone can perform the duty, then that service is dispensable. What musicians provide in churches is in high demand and low supply. Therefore, they should be paid.

BIBLICAL PRECEDENCE

Frequently we levy conjecture when the Bible is replete as to what should be done given any situation that arises concerning ministry. Musicians and whether they should be compensated fits with the niche of this model. What does the Word of God say about the musicians?

First, we have to establish who the Levites are? Traditionally, it's been communicated that Levites include singers, band members, and ministers. However, the Holy Scriptures suggest otherwise. Nehemiah, who was a forward thinker, distinguished the differences between positions. He suggested:

> And then I learned that the Levites hadn't been given their regular food allotments. So the Levites and singers who led the services of worship had all left and gone back to their farms. I called the officials on the carpet,
>
> "Why has The Temple of God been abandoned?" I got everyone back again and put them back on their jobs so that all Judah was again bringing in the tithe of grain, wine, and oil to the storerooms.

> – Nehemiah 13:10–13 (The Message)

Notice the distinction between Levites and musicians. Additionally, notice that those in charge of music were pooled together and described biblically as musicians or singers. We understand what is predicated upon the text; the Levites, who were of the Tribe of Levi, were dedicated a portion of what came into the temple. Nehemiah expands on the notion that there was a portion designated for the musicians as well. The part according to Nehemiah included grain, wine, and oil. These items, like money today, were the mediums of exchange. Therefore, it is documented that musicians can be compensated for their worshipful gifts.

Additionally, we find in scripture that musicians worked "all hours." First Chronicles entail that musicians were exempt from other church duties since they were on a mission at all hours (I Chronicles 9:33). We can safely deduce that an Old Testament musician wasn't just there on Sundays, Wednesdays, and rehearsals. They put in the work and therefore received compensation based on their contribution.

PAY ME

Recently, I had an incident where I had to call in a national company called "Critter control." I needed to get the guy to set traps and do whatever it took to relieve us of the unwanted guest. As we sat and conversed, I asked the gentleman what it would cost for his services. The price came out to be close to one thousand dollars. Personally, I didn't care what the costs were. I needed this creature out! I asked him, for the sake of reference, what the job was going to cost. He said, "The material is only about one hundred dollars." He indicated that most of his cost was composed of labor. He said something I would never forget. He said, "Pastor Rich, I have a Master's in wildlife. There are not many people around who can do what I do."

Enough said! People like him go to school for years to charge what they do in minutes because it's their expertise. Musicians are no different. As Pastors, we must recognize their importance and ensure that they are fairly compensated.

RICH WISDOM

I didn't want to close the chapters without contributing wisdom to the Pastors in their dealings with the musicians. Without over twenty years in ministry and ten in the pastorate, I believe there are some things to consider when developing an excellent worship atmosphere. These items that I advise upon are not all-inclusive, but ones that every Pastor should consider.

Consider a Contract or Memorandum of Understanding (MOU)
Anything that's not in writing is not real. Each band member or contractor should sign a memorandum of understanding to display what to expect from us, pay scale, what we expect from them, and their job

duties as agreed upon. The paperwork becomes a point of reference to refer to in case there is some misunderstanding or miscommunication that could ensue during the contractor or employee's tenure.

Consider an Interview

Often Pastors will place people in position simply to fill a void. As a result, we get someone who brings gifts to the table but doesn't have the character to stay there. Chemistry and culture is also an essential factor to consider during the interview. A person may be Holy and have the skillset but won't mesh well with the culture of the church or the chemistry of the existing members. An interview gives the Pastor and the musician an idea of the type of atmosphere to expect when working with the worship department. I also encourage musicians to sit through a couple of worship services so that they can get an idea of what it's like during actual service.

Pay Them What You Can Afford

A chief complaint from musicians is that they are not adequately paid or the checks bounce. For the Pastor reading this work, to give someone a check when the money is not in the bank is called lying. Bouncing a check is a sin. Period! I understand things happen in ministry, but it's essential to meet your obligations the way you promised. If I promised a three-hundred-dollar check, then a hundred dollars and gift cards will not be good enough. Get a clear understanding of what it will take to maintain that musician and act accordingly to what you agreed upon. Ensure that the agreement is in writing.

Negotiate on Equipment

Top musicians typically have quality equipment. High-quality equipment could mean that the person spent thousands to ensure they have premium equipment. If a Pastor requires a musician to bring their own equipment, then that band membership should be paid more than a fair market rate. If the church provides the equipment, then the band members should take that into consideration.

Establish Fair Compensation

To establish fair compensation, one must research the marketable salary for that position. There are also bodies of written works and companies that can assist with the endeavor of establishing wages for musicians. I would advise a Pastor to exercise due diligence. Additionally, ensure that the musician feels comfortable with the offered salary.

Emphasize Spirituality

We've spoken about the business affairs concerning musicians and their recruitment. Often, we forget that what we partake in is hugely spiritual. In times past, I witnessed musicians and singers who performed well, but there wasn't any spirituality in their service. In the church, we call it an anointing. The anointing allows burdens to lift and destroy yokes. Expect your musicians to participate in service. Expect them to know how to pray. Expect them to be active participants in the word. A performance moves crowds, but an anointing moves chains.

A PERFORMANCE MOVES CROWDS, BUT AN ANOINTING MOVES CHAINS.

We have to learn to marry the two disciplines. Synergy is defined when people come together to produce a more significant effect than the individual parts. We are better together. Whether you are a musician or Pastor reading this work, understand that any relationship requires compromise. We must avoid dangerous comparisons. The friend who serves at another church situation may be different. The Pastor down the street's budget may be more extensive. As people who are charged with speaking the gospel, we must put aside our differences and keep a higher purpose in mind. Together, we can advance the Kingdom and win souls for God.

HELP IS ON THE WAY!

The purpose of life is not to be happy. It is to be useful,
to be honorable, to be compassionate, to have it make
some difference that you have lived and lived well.

— *Ralph Waldo Emerson*

Throughout the book, we have exposed problems and issues that exist within the confines of the pastorate. It was my complete intention to convince the reader that burdens exist. Many of those who dove into the confines of the book are parishioners serving under the auspices of a ministry gift. Now that you are aware of the pains that Pastors endure, I would be remiss to not advise the readers how to uphold and uplift the arms of your leaders.

YOUR PASTOR IS HUMAN

The Book of Exodus tells a poignant story of a weary leader named Moses. Moses, who experienced some of the greatest successes in the biblical narrative. He pastored more people than any other person in antiquity and modernity. He was the leader of leaders. The biblical text illustrates a leader who was without a perfect record. Although he has the legend of deity, the Bible painted a picture of a mortal man who had sensitive issues and a few insecurities. He had Superman qualities but deep down, he was Clark Kent. The first approach to helping your Pastor is to realize that they are human. Depending on your position in the church, you may have the opportunity to work closely with the Pastor. You'll see Clark Kent often. As a person working near the Pastor, you must keep this in the recesses of your mind. Pastors struggle with the same struggles with which others wrestle. However, the intensity is like the highest level of massage TENS unit. The enemy understands that if I cut off the head, the body will wander. As Pastors, we are gifted spiritually, but that doesn't negate the issues with the flesh. We make mistakes, but the world and those in the church have donated their lives to magnifying the mistakes of the Pastor. We live in a bubble. Our lives are on display as if we live aquatic lives. What if news outlets viewed your personal philosophies and statements on Facebook as an official statement from the church as an organization? What if your every movement was judged like issues in People's Court? The fallacy of how people think Pastors should be are often in conflict with how we really are. We like to joke. We have proclivities and insecurities. We have weak moments where working for God overrides our worship of Him. The glaring issue is that we get to hear about all of your mistakes and advise accordingly—but when you hear about ours, you leave the church.

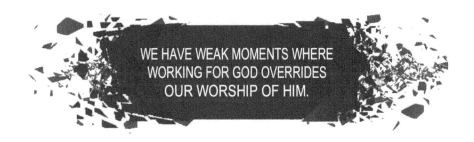

WE HAVE WEAK MOMENTS WHERE WORKING FOR GOD OVERRIDES OUR WORSHIP OF HIM.

Members must make a conscious effort to remind themselves that their Pastor is human. They will bleed the same blood and partake in the same grave experience. The only difference is that the Pastor has to carry the mantle of God's covenant while fighting the battles of carnality. Yes, your Pastor makes it looks natural. They seem to balance church and family. The first family seems to have all the amenities afforded to the upper echelon of the erudite aristocracy. Their children are perfect little creatures who seem to gravitate to biblical principles better than the average child. At this point, take your right hand, lift it in the air, and proceed to strike your right cheek! You must wake up! The reality is that Pastors are fighting to find a balance between spending time with family and the church. They have functions at the same times that other important events take place. Pastor's flesh fights like two opposing teams on Monday Night Football. Sometimes the Pastor and spouse have heated arguments right before getting up to speak with the anointing of the Holy Spirit. She smiles to keep from cussing or to cover the sailor-like serenade she gave him before his feeble spiritual dissertation. Pastors' kids have the track records of making some of the dumbest decisions out of rebellion and purposeful misrepresentation of the first family. The only difference between the Pastor and parishioner is that the Pastor's failures, indiscretions, and human flaws often get accentuated in public spaces.

The heat from the spotlight often serves as a torch melting away the wax of expectation. Underneath the thick cloak of high hope and immortal misrepresentation lies a man or woman of God who is both extraordinarily flawed and as equally gifted. The unique dichotomy and conflict of two natures leave members of the judging public to believe that their Pastor presented a lie to the whole relationship. The truth is your Pastor is called to be like Jesus, but they are not Jesus. The fallacy of misplacement of humanity often leaves members crushed and broken. Those reading this text must understand that the Pastor must conflate the flesh and the spirit just like everyone else. They fight emotional and mental wars but often of higher intensity. Your Pastor is human. A well-known Pastor told me recently that members can come into our office and tell us about their indiscretions. We're charged to

YOUR PASTOR IS HUMAN.

keep a straight face and a non-judgmental stance. However, when they hear that their leader is not a perfect person, they judge the Pastor, when their leader extended to them the olive branch of grace. It's tragic, but its roots are inculcated with the truth. Yes, a Pastor is supposed to live above the fray. But let me ask, how did you fail? How did you make a mistake? Did you plan it? Neither do we. A combination of fits of carnality, seasons of prayerlessness, business over devotion, weariness from fighting, encumbrances from administrating church work, drowning in others' problems—a Pastor must swim through the abyss of their personal issues while carrying the weight that comes with pastoring. Your Pastor is human; therefore, change your perspective and increase your compassion. Please pay careful attention to this next section, as I offer some simple action steps that will enhance the relationship and the connection with your leader.

PRAY FOR THEM

Before you skip over this section because it sounds like some old cliché command that you heard growing up in church, hear me out. Prayer is a rudimentary principle in the Christian faith. One could assume that just because one identifies with the faith, that they practice the principle. Very few Christians engage in this fundamental practice. Every distraction from social media to busyness claims victims continuously. If Christians are not praying for themselves, it's safe to assume they are slacking in praying for their Pastors. In the natural sense, it's difficult to talk about someone you are praying for. Our critical view of someone disallows us to engage in the spiritual combat for that person.

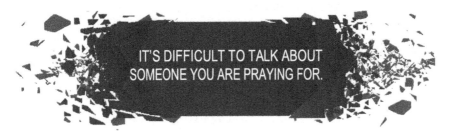

IT'S DIFFICULT TO TALK ABOUT SOMEONE YOU ARE PRAYING FOR.

Additionally, praying for your Pastor is an indication of honor. Scripture indicates that we should give recognition to whom honor is due. Prayer honors your Pastor. It means that their well-being, albeit it spiritual or existential, crosses your mind. A good member becomes a great prayer warrior for their Pastor. They understand the demand and the destruction that pulls upon their Pastor. I encourage those who are gazing at this text to pray for others. Pray for your Pastor that they become the shepherd who continues to help develop your soul and the souls of others.

DOUBLE HONOR

Honoring your Pastor is one of the greatest acts of love a member can make. No matter what's the size of their church or what you think are the sizes of their pockets, they need resources. Honor them with money and other gifts. Whether they tell you or not, they need it. I grew up in an era where it was a great tradition to honor the Pastor with Pastoral Anniversaries. The people were requested to pay assessments during the allotted time of the year. Back when I was growing up, it wasn't strange for a small church of fewer than fifty people to raise fifty thousand dollars for their Pastor. The people would inundate them with gifts such as toilet paper, paper products, detergent, and other household cleaning supplies. Earlier this year, a young lady gave us a basket of supplies. The feeling we had was amazing! As a result, my wife now buys some of the detergent that the basket contained.

There many ways to honor your Pastor. Think about the things that are required to operate your life. Often, those are the same things that are needed in the Pastor's household. Think about how you would want someone to respond if your name was mentioned maliciously. Think about how it makes you feel to get honored. Honor means something of value or weight. If your Pastor is vital to you, treat them and their family as people of importance.

RUNNING WITH VISION

If you're reading this book, either you are a Pastor who has a destination or a parishioner who is following a Pastor to a destination. The question remains, "What are you doing to help your Pastor get to that destination?" When the Pastor casts vision, scripture doesn't tell him to fulfill it alone. Habakkuk concisely articulates this notion that each person who reads it, should run with it:

> Then the LORD answered me and said,
> "Record the vision
> And inscribe it on tablets,
> That the one who reads it may run.
> "For the vision is yet for the appointed time;
> It hastens toward the goal and it will not fail.
> Though it tarries, wait for it;
> For it will certainly come, it will not delay."

–Habakkuk 2:2–3 (NASB95)

It goes on to inform the reader that the vision will not fail. Why? Those who read it will fulfill it. As a member, it is your responsibility to familiarize yourself with vision, see where you fit, and accomplish your portion. When a church runs with the vision, it creates synergy. Aristotle didn't coin the philosophy but popularized it. He indicated that the whole is greater than the sum of the parts. We are greater together. A church where each person does their part will accomplish great and mighty feats.

For the Pastors reading this text, it is your responsibility to make the vision clear, concise, and available to carry. Vision casting is so important that authors like Samuel Chand dedicated entire works to get Pastors to dedicate time and effort in vision casting. I highly recommend books by Dr. Chand such as *Who's Holding Your Ladder?* and *Laddershifts*. I've learned that if people are not moving, it may be an indication that the vision is unclear. Pastor, you may stop and slow down to recalibrate your ministry vision and improve your vision casting. Additionally, asking for help doesn't mean you're helpless. As Pastors, we must assess our strengths and weaknesses, but ultimately, we must drop the ball so others can pick up. We must lose our pride and allow others to handle rudimentary matters.

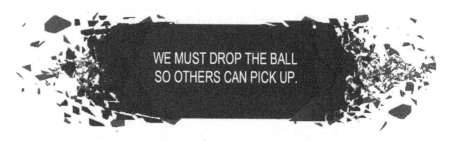

WE MUST DROP THE BALL
SO OTHERS CAN PICK UP.

The Pastor must use all the available wisdom at their disposal. Knowing you have people who can pick up the weight but choosing to do it yourself is a manifestation of pride. I've had many seasons of pride. It leads to depression, burnout, and outright anger. I've had numbers to well-renowned Pastors and ministers across the world that I didn't use. Pride stopped me from using them. Sometimes we can access a hammer but we choose to hang the picture with the shoe. A great story that exemplifies this principle is found in Exodus:

> Moses' father-in-law Jethro, along with Moses' wife and sons, came to him in the wilderness where he was camped at the mountain of God. He sent word to Moses, "I, your father-in-law Jethro, am coming to you with your wife and her two sons."
>
> The next day Moses sat down to judge the people, and they stood around Moses from morning until evening. When Moses' father-in-law saw everything he was doing for them he asked, "What is this thing you're doing for the

people? Why are you alone sitting as judge, while all the people stand around you from morning until evening?"

Moses replied to his father-in-law, "Because the people come to me to inquire of God. Whenever they have a dispute, it comes to me, and I make a decision between one man and another. I teach them God's statutes and laws." "What you're doing is not good," Moses' father-in-law said to him. "You will certainly wear out both yourself and these people who are with you because the task is too heavy for you. You can't do it alone."

– Exodus 18:5–6; 13-18 (HCSB)

Notice at the beginning of the passage, Moses' wife and two sons were with Jethro at the onset and with him as they watched Moses work. Moses was married to a Cushite woman. Do you think that his wife never mentioned to Moses that he was doing too much? I can hear the Cushite rolling her neck like an African American woman telling him, "Moses, you're doing too much. Moses, you're spending too much time at the church. Moses, let someone else do it." My wife, as that Cushite reminds me, always says that I must delegate more. The question remains, why did it take Jethro to come and tell Moses what I'm assuming those around him echoed? Sometimes we don't accept wisdom from people who are close to us because their voices have become familiar to us. There are jewels of resources at our disposal. Sometimes they don't look like something we would use, but Samson used the jawbone of the ass to slay thousands. Unconventional, but it's what God provided at the time. As leaders, we should be open to hearing wisdom even if we are the ones who give it most of the time. Don't miss a wife or Jethro moment because we are caught up in the vessel that God uses to deliver it.

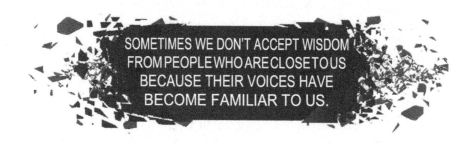

SOMETIMES WE DON'T ACCEPT WISDOM FROM PEOPLE WHO ARE CLOSE TO US BECAUSE THEIR VOICES HAVE BECOME FAMILIAR TO US.

GIVING

Giving, like prayer, is a keystone topic in Christendom. The churches need your assistance to help fulfill the vision God gave them. Your love and prayers are great, but it doesn't keep the lights on. It doesn't help with church utilities. It doesn't help the Pastor alleviate financial stress. Money is the medium of exchange. There are missions, locally and abroad, that need your attention, but the primary mission starts at home. When Pastors don't have to concern themselves with finances, they can give more time to prayer and study.

Additionally, giving helps provide for the community. Biblically, people contributed to ensuring that the needs of others are met. The day I wrote this section, we received six calls for benevolence. If parishioners in my church didn't give, we wouldn't be able to assist those who needed emergency assistance. I challenge those who are reading this book to develop a habit of giving. If you don't believe your churches manage finances well, then change churches!

SERVING

A church is a nonprofit. Like any other nonprofit, it thrives off charitable donations and volunteerism. Although churches have different cultures, understand that the majority of churches survive because of people donating their time. In many circles, people feel they need to get paid for everything. If you must get paid for everything, you're not a volunteer, you're an employee. Churches across the country have been able to break growth barriers because people who are skilled in their craft donated their time instead of churches paying for outside services. Imagine if the electrician helped the church during an electrical emergency, or the plumber doing likewise. Imagine a young freelance graphic designer donating his time to the church but charging those on the outside. The synergy from working with the ministry to alleviate cost can cause your church to become bigger, better, and brighter. I want to encourage readers to begin to think about how you can help bring your skills to use for the Glory of God.

CONSISTENT ATTENDANCE

The twenty-first century is experiencing a renaissance in technology. Screens are everywhere. Google has revolutionized the way people find information and placed encyclopedias on the extinction list. There are numerous positives which I could accentuate; however with every positive, there is a potential negative. The internet brought a visceral attack on the butts in the seats.

Statistically, church attendance is down across the country. Why? It's not rocket science. I can sit in the confines of my home and have praise and worship with the most dynamic praise team in the country. I may not like the preaching of that church, so I can log off and join the live stream of my favorite preacher across the country. Well, that preacher may raise extensive offerings and so, at my discretion, I don't have to lift a finger to dismiss myself. I simply click the close button and go about my daily tasks. I'm not necessarily instructed to give or participate in an altar call. I don't have to be concerned with what I have on. I can sit in front of my device with a bonnet and be free without judgment. Sounds ideal, doesn't it?

To articulate this concept in a simplistic way, not coming to church is like watching a movie on a DVD. You'll get the content. You'll see the film, but it is not the same as being in the theater. The theater brings a different experience. Right now, millions of ministries have swamped online because of an menacing pandemic. We are able to reach people, get them saved, but it's not the same. The aura is created through socialization. The kids get an opportunity to learn on their level and have fun while doing it. You get to do life together. I'm in no way suggesting that streaming service is all bad, but what I am suggesting is that it shouldn't be your first option. Maybe you were scheduled to work one day. Perhaps you're traveling but don't want to miss an enlightening sermon. It's understandable, but the truth is the Pastor wants and needs your presence. He needs your encouragement. He needs the essence you bring to the sanctuary. You're a part of the extended family, and Sundays and midweek services are the family reunions. If you never come, the Pastor doesn't get to see your kids grow. He doesn't get to hear the many testimonies of what God has performed in your life. The Pastor doesn't get to hug your necks and shake your hands. These are the little things that make a Pastor smile. Those of you reading this book make a conscious effort to commit to consistent attendance.

Your Pastor needs you just like you need him or her. The synergy created from working together to advance the mission and the vision of the church can impact neighborhoods, cities, governments, and even nations. Take what you've read to heart and try to get consistent with each category. There are other things that a member can do to assist the Pastor, but start with these and watch how God moves in your life and the lives of other believers!

FINAL THOUGHT

Honesty is the first chapter in the book of wisdom.

— Thomas Jefferson

Pastors are facing dire times. The church at large is on a decline. The Bible talks about the great falling away. Therefore, we shouldn't be surprised by this trend. The decline in attendance has left Pastors feeling rejected, unaccomplished, and depressed, especially those who pastorate is their vocation and occupation. The churches across the world are under attack. In America, hundreds of churches are permanently closing their doors and Pastors are walking away to do other things. The notion of closing churches is not to suggest that the ones that close their doors should be open, but the body of Christ is losing great Pastors and ministries that could have had impacted their space.

The world needs the church. I recall significant calamities in the early twenty-first century. We've had devastating storms like Hurricane

Katrina that ravaged New Orleans. We've witnessed shattering earth-
quakes that rocked Haiti in 2010. Many of our Puerto Rican brothers are
still recovering from the savage destruction of Hurricane Maria. When
one gazes at old new coverage, we see a constant body of people at each
calamity: The church. Institutions like the Catholic Church are rocked
with scandals. It seems like weekly that a church or another Pastor is in
the spotlight for something they may or may not have done. The details
don't matter to parasitic people. They feast from the fact that it made
the news headlines and they get to cast more doubt upon the crippled
institution. The church has never been, and never will be, perfect. In
fact, if you do find a perfect church, don't join it, because when you do, it
ceases to be perfect. The church is made up of imperfect people carrying
out His perfect will. Despite its imperfections, the church is present. The
church was present during each natural disaster and terrorist event. The
church was there during the burial of your mother or father. The church
was there when your budget failed to cover your bills. The church was
there in the wake of devastation in your marriage. The counsel from
the Pastor or staff helped to resurrect a dead relationship. The church
was there when you got the doctor's report that changed the course of
your life. The church was there for the new birth of your bundle of joy
that you believed God to bring into this world. The church was there
for your greatest joys and your deepest pains. Even during one of the
greatest calamities of our time, the church will be here to help people
and even the government to pick up pieces.

Is she perfect? No, the local church never will perfect but she will
always be there. The local church is not your favorite internet Pastor who
in all honesty, is not praying for you. They can't be there for any of the
events named above. They can't be there for any of your child's pivotal
moments. You need the local church. I encourage each person reading
this book to connect with one. You may differ in political ideology. You

may have differences of opinion on taboo topics, but find commonality and get planted. Find a church that can utilize your skillset and benefit from your presence. The local church can be great again! It needs you. It needs people like you who took the time to understand the plight and the pain of the Pastor.

I purposely didn't use a lot of stats although the Sociology Professor in me would have obliged. I wanted you to hear from a Pastor about a Pastor who covers Pastors and talks to Pastors across the country. I listen to their cries and complaints. I am a shoulder that they cry upon when they want to choke members or just vent. I've been a listening ear to those who have been betrayed by those who are close to them. The pain of pastoring is the cross that many pastors bear.

As we close our long conversation, you must contribute to the solution. Tell your Pastor that you appreciate them. Tell them that you support their vision. Place some money in their hands and not just on the anniversary. They need your time, your talent, and your treasure. Lastly, and most importantly, pray for them. I echo the sentiments that it's hard to talk about those whom you're praying for. They need the strength of God to fulfill the obligation of a Pastor. They need God to touch them. We believe that there is strength in agreement. God bless you, and it is my prayer and heartfelt desire that you got something from this book.

BIBLIOGRAPHY

Barna, George. *The State of Pastors: How Today's Faith Leaders Are Navigating Life and Leadership in an Age of Complexity.* Research Report in conjunction with Pepperdine University, 2017. All data from this source.

Cloud, Henry, Dr., Townsend, John, Dr. *The Mom Factor.* Zondervan, 1998.

Morris, Leon L. *Luke: An Introduction and Commentary.* WMB Eerdmans Publishing, 1988.

The New American Standard Bible (NASB). The Lockman Foundation, P.O. Box 2279, La Habra, CA 90631.

"Perfection." In *Merriam-Webster.com.* Retrieved January 15, 2020 from https://www.merriam-webster.com/dictionary/perfection.

Peterson, Eugene H. *The Message: The Bible in Contemporary Language.* NavPress, 2002.

Rainer, Thom. 2012. "Five Things You Should Know About Pastors' Salaries." In Thom Rainer, *Growing Healthy Churches Together.* [Online] December 17, 2012.

Vernon, Rainnel. *Help, My Pastor Is Under Pressure: How Leaders Can Help Their Pastor Succeed.* Cleveland, Ohio, Victory Media & Publishing, 2018.

Made in the USA
Monee, IL
17 November 2020